A Systemic Functional Grammar of French

A Systemic Functional Grammar of French provides an accessible introduction to systemic functional linguistics through French.

This concise introduction to the systemic functional grammar (SFG) framework provides illustrations throughout that highlight how the framework can be used to analyse authentic language texts.

This will be of interest to students in alternative linguistic frameworks who wish to acquire a basic understanding of SFG as well as academics in related areas, such as literary and cultural studies, interested in seeing how SFG can be applied to their fields.

David Banks is Emeritus Professor of English Linguistics at Université de Bretagne Occidentale, France.

A Systemic Functional Grammar of French

A Simple Introduction

David Banks

LONDON AND NEW YORK

First published 2017 by Routledge

2 Park Square, Milton Park, Abingdon, Oxfordshire OX14 4RN
52 Vanderbilt Avenue, New York, NY 10017

Routledge is an imprint of the Taylor & Francis Group, an informa business

First issued in paperback 2020

British Library Cataloguing-in-Publication Data
A catalogue record for this book is available from the British Library

Library of Congress Cataloging-in-Publication Data
A catalog record for this book has been requested

ISBN: 978-0-415-78514-3 (hbk)
ISBN: 978-0-367-60742-5 (pbk)

Typeset in Times New Roman
by Apex CoVantage, LLC

Contents

Author's note

No-one writes a book without becoming indebted to a great number of people. This book has been written over a long period, often in short spurts, but has gradually built up over the years. Originally it was intended to be a collaborative effort, with three co-authors supplying drafts on different parts, and criticizing and correcting each others' work. As it happened, my colleagues became involved in other, no less interesting projects, and, ultimately, I have ended up writing the whole book myself. Nevertheless, the two colleagues in question, Janet Ormrod and Chris Gledhill, have been a constant source of encouragement and constructive criticism, for which they have my heartfelt thanks. It is with their agreement that I am now publishing this book in its present form. In addition to them, there are the innumerable colleagues and students who over the years, and even decades, have contributed, often unwittingly, to the way I conceived of language in general, and the French language in particular. I thank them all, though it is obviously impossible to list them, though I hope that some will recognize themselves in these few lines.

1 By way of introduction

Language is a fascinating phenomenon. We use it constantly, every day, to communicate, and it would be difficult to conceive of human existence without it. Yet, at the same time, we would be hard put to say what it is. In fact, it is so closely bound up with our everyday lives that usually we don't even bother to think about it. Linguistics, the academic discipline that does attempt to think about language, and ask questions about its nature, is peculiar. In other disciplines, we use language to talk about other things. In linguistics, we use language to talk about language itself. The object of study is also the means of communicating whatever we know or find out about it. On the other hand, since language is such an integral part of our everyday lives, which we all use constantly, everyone and anyone seems to feel free and able to make pronouncements about it, which can frequently be frustrating for those who have spent a lot of time and energy trying to come to terms with this complex phenomenon. Indeed, the more one looks into this subject, the more complex it seems to become. This may be true of all forms of research. The image I have frequently used of the researcher is that of a person who studies a grain of sand year after year, attempting to understand it from all angles. After many, many years he thinks he has just about understood his grain of sand, and it is at that moment that he looks up and sees the beach! Even so, he still thinks his years of endeavour were worth the effort.

There are numerous ways of approaching language, but I feel that they all fall into one of three main categories. I shall call these categories formal, cognitive, and functional. Formal theories, as the name implies, are those that treat language basically as a question of form. This is what most people would think of as grammar and syntax, and formal linguists would claim that everything that is interesting about language can be said in terms of grammar and syntax. Anything that goes beyond this, they would consider to be relatively subjective and not particularly serious, from an academic point of view. The most well-known theories of this type are those based on the work of Noam Chomsky, who has the distinction of coming as close as a linguist ever comes to becoming a household name. Since this approach deals with language as form, and much of the work consists in moving the forms around to form the different structural possibilities of a language, I often think of it as the Lego theory of language. Cognitive theories are those that attempt to discover the mental processes that occur when we communicate. Such theories became popular in the United States in the late-twentieth century, and have since spread to many other places. A particular, and separate, brand of cognitive linguistics has evolved in France, based on the work of Benveniste, and developed notably by Culioli. This French approach usually goes under the name of *théorie de l'énonciation.* The third category is that of functional approaches to language, which attempt to discover how languages work. This is the type of approach that interests me and that will be used in this book. There are many different types of functional approach, but the one that I find suits my purposes best is Systemic Functional Linguistics. This theory is based on the work of Michael Halliday. The origins of Halliday's approach can be found in earlier work, notably that of his own teacher Firth; to this he incorporated ideas borrowed from the Prague School of linguistics. The fact that I find this approach the most useful for my purposes does not mean that the others are in any sense "wrong"; they are simply attempting to do rather different things. Consequently, different linguistic theories should be seen as being complementary, rather than in opposition. If one compares Halliday's approach with cognitive approaches, they can be seen as starting from opposing viewpoints, but converging on the same object. Halliday has said that while Systemic Functional Linguistics starts from language in order to move towards cognition, cognitive approaches start from cognition to move towards language. So they are on the same road, albeit starting from diametrically opposed points, and travelling in opposite directions; presumably they should meet somewhere in the middle! Formal approaches are somewhat different, but all approaches have to deal with form at some point since language is always realised as form, whether it is as sound or in some visual form.

Systemic Functional Linguistics is functional in two slightly different senses. First it is interested in the way a language functions internally; that is, how the different elements that go to make up the language work together to create meaning. Secondly, it is interested in the way a language functions externally. That is, how it functions in society, as a way of creating meaning in human communication.

This explains why the theory is functional, but it is also systemic. The term "systemic" is derived from "system", but here system refers to the network of choices that are available to the speaker of a language. These are the resources of the language that are available to him when he sets out to communicate something to someone else. If at some point in the creation of the communication the decision has been made to use a noun, then it automatically follows that the noun must be either countable or uncountable. It must be one or the other; there are no other possibilities. If countable is chosen, then it automatically follows that one must then choose between singular or plural. Again, it must be one or the other and there are no other possibilities. This can be represented as follows:

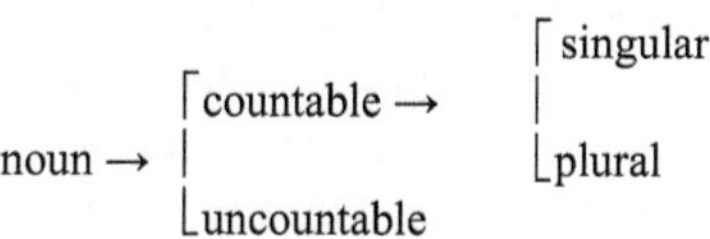

Or, to take another example, if we are at the point of making a decision about the mood of a clause, then the choice must be made between indicative and imperative. If indicative is chosen, then the further choice must be made between declarative and interrogative:

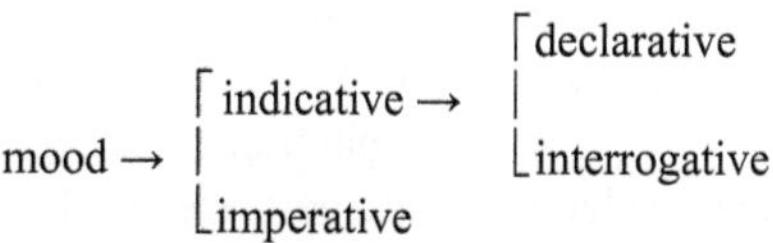

In theory, the whole of the grammar of a language would form a single, though highly complex, system network, of which the two tiny snippets above would form parts. By this we do not mean that the speaker consciously goes through these stages; this is obviously not true. But it is intended to represent the network of choices, the resources that are available in a particular language. One of the peculiarities of the system network is that as we move through the system from left to right, we are making choices that are more and more detailed, or "delicate". And the final, most detailed, most delicate, choice to be made is one about lexis, the actual words that are chosen to encode the communication. Many theories make a fairly stark distinction between grammar and the lexicon, or list of words that are available in a language. In Systemic Functional Linguistics, grammar and the lexis are part of the same system, which is why we often refer to "lexicogrammar".

The lexicogrammar is perhaps the most central, immediate, visible part of the language. But it exists as a means of realizing or encoding meanings. The meanings it expresses are the semantic level of the language. Systemic Functional Linguistics distinguishes three different types of meaning, usually referred to as metafunctions. The ideational metafunction deals with the way in which we represent the world around us and the inner world of our thoughts and feelings. For example, this would involve processes, usually encoded in lexicogrammar as verbs, and the participants involved in those processes, usually encoded at the lexicogrammatical level as nouns. The interpersonal metafunction deals with the relationships established by the speaker. These relationships can be either between the speaker and the message he is communicating, or between the speaker and the person he is communicating with. It therefore involves such features as mood and modality. The third metafunction is the textual metafunction, and this deals with the way in which the message is structured: what the elements are that begin or end the clause and why. Although we can only talk about one of the metafunctions at a time, and may sometimes be particularly interested in only one of them, it should always be remembered that none of them are any more important than the others; they all have equal importance, and all three are always present in any piece of language.

Systemic Functional Linguistics insists on the fact that language is a social phenomenon. It always exists within a particular social environment from which it emanates. Thus, language depends on the context in which it is created, but once created it becomes part of that context, which is thus modified; so there is a constant process of mutual creation between the context and language. The immediate context is frequently called register, and this can be analysed in terms of three functions: field, tenor and mode. Field is the activity of which the language is a part. Tenor refers to the relationship between those taking part in the language activity. And mode is the method by which the message is communicated; in its simplest form this distinguishes between spoken and written language. Beyond register is the more general context, or context of culture, for which some use the term genre.

Systemic Functional Linguistics has never been a closed, fixed way of thinking. It has always been open to variations and alternatives. This is indeed part of its attraction, though it may sometimes be disconcerting for the beginning student or the person new to this field. Michael Halliday has sometimes talked about the different "dialects" of the theory. The version presented in this book is fairly close to the most usual version of the theory, though at some points it does bear some personal traits. However, readers who go on to read other books about Systemic Functional Linguistics should not be surprised to find minor differences in both content and terminology.

In the sections that follow, there are four that are fairly extensive, dealing with lexicogrammatical functions and the three semantic metafunctions – ideational, interpersonal, and textual. These are followed by three fairly short sections, introducing register, grammatical metaphor, and Appraisal Theory. All the examples used are genuine, in the sense that they are taken from real life. They actually occurred in authentic documents. Moreover, since this book is intended to show how Systemic Functional Linguistics applies to modern French, all the examples come from texts that appeared in the twenty-first century. So, this book presents a systemic grammar of twenty-first-century French. Throughout there are analyses of extended authentic examples, which are from genuine texts of the twenty-first century. It has been my intention to keep this book as simple as possible, without, I hope, becoming simplistic. I hope that this will give the reader the desire to go on to find out more about the theory, what it can do, and how it can be used. For this reason, these sections are followed by some suggestions for further reading. One of the difficulties of such reading lists is that they are out of date as soon as they appear since new books are appearing all the time; but that cannot be helped, and I hope that the suggestions will nevertheless enable the reader to go beyond this book.

2 Encoding language

Lexicogrammatical functions

In this chapter, we will see how clauses are made up of groups, and groups are themselves made up of words. We will see that there are different kinds of clauses, groups, and words. We will also consider how one type of unit can function as a unit at a different level, in a process that is called rankshift.

2.1 Groups

The basic unit of a text is the clause. The clause is made up of one or more groups. These groups are of four types: subject, predicator, complement, and circumstantial adjunct. Although there are other kinds of adjunct, the circumstantial adjunct is the most common, so when we talk about an "adjunct", without further specification, this means the circumstantial adjunct. The predicator is encoded in language by a verbal group; a subject is the element that is primarily involved in the event or state described by the predicator, and can be probed by the question "who or what?" followed by the verb in question. The complement is the item that is secondarily involved in the event or state, and it can be probed by the question formed by the subject followed by the verb, then "who or what?". The adjunct gives the circumstances of the event or state. Thus, in the following clause:

(1) Ils ont fêté Noël sur Twitter.

(*Femme Actuelle*, 9–15 janvier 2012)

The predicator is encoded by the verb *ont fêté*. If we ask "who or what *ont fêté* something?" the pronoun *ils* gives us the answer. This is the subject. If we then ask "*Ils ont fêté* what?" the answer is *Noël*. This is the complement. Circumstantial questions, like where? when? why? how? give us the adjunct, in this case, *sur Twitter*. Using S, P, C, and A as symbols for subject, predicator, complement and adjunct, this could be analysed as follows:

S	P	C	A
Ils	ont fêté	Noël	sur Twitter

2.2 Words

Each group is made up of one or more words. Consider the following extract:

> (2) Vu le nombre de grossesses non désirées d'IVG chez les jeunes filles mineures, le Pass Contraception se généralise à la rentrée dans les lycées de plusieurs régions de France.
>
> (*Elle*, 16 septembre 2011)

This contains the nominal group *les jeunes filles mineures*. This group contains four words. One of these is easily recognizable as the main, or central, word of this group, to which the others are attached; this is the word *filles*. We call this the head, symbolized by a (lower-case) h. The other words in the group give us more information about the head, in this case, *jeunes* about age, and *mineures* about legal status. Where such words occur to the left of the head we call them modifiers (symbolized by m); where they occur to the right, they are called qualifiers (symbolized by q). Thus, *jeunes* is a modifier, and *mineures* is a qualifier. In one sense, it would have been possible to give both of these the same name, since they have the same function, that of describing the head. The difference is one of position in the group and not of function. However, in practice, it is useful to have separate names for those that occur before and after the head. In French, the majority of describing words and phrases function as qualifiers rather than modifiers, but there are exceptions such as *jeunes* in this example. This group also contains the word *les*. This also gives information about the head, albeit information of a different type. This type of word is often called a determiner, and such words always occur to the left of the head. Although many books consider determiners to be a separate kind of word, for the purposes of this simple introduction, determiners will be considered to be a special type of modifier. So, our nominal group, *les jeunes filles mineures*, would be analysed as follows.

m	m	h	q
les	jeunes	filles	mineures

This type of structure, a head preceded by one or more modifiers (or none), and followed by one or more qualifiers (or none), is typical of nominal groups. However, sometimes other groups may have this type of structure too. Thus, in the following example:

> (3) Il rétablit une frontière très nette entre “bouffe de garçon” et “cuisine de fille”.
>
> (*Elle*, 16 septembre 2011)

the qualifier *nette* is preceded by *très*. The group formed by *très nette* can be analysed as a head preceded by a modifier:

m	h
très	nette

Verbal groups, on the other hand, have a different type of structure. Consider the following example:

> (4) La crise de l’euro et les déboires d’Angela Merkel ont relégué au second plan la vie politique berlinoise.
>
> (*Le Monde*, 13 december 2011)

The verbal group, *ont relégué*, is made up of two elements; the second of these, *relégué*, describes the action, event or state that is taking place. This will be called the verb, symbolized by v. The first element gives information about other verbal characteristics such as aspect. This will be called the auxiliary, symbolized by a. We presume that the use of the traditional terms “verb” and “auxiliary” as technical labels here will surprise no-one. Thus, this verbal group would be analysed as follows:

a	v
ont	relégué

However, consider the verbal group in the following extract:

> (5) Le prix remis s’applique immédiatement aux achats des étudiants et lycéens sur TOUS LES RAYONS.
>
> (Fidelity card leaflet, 2012)

It will be seen that the verb has the word *se* (here reduced to *s’*) attached to it. Traditionally, this has been called a reflexive pronoun. However, only in a minority of cases can this really be treated as a pronoun (Banks 2009a,

2010a). In the case illustrated here, it would be difficult to treat *se* as a pronoun. In many cases, it is totally impossible to do so:

(6) En pratique, il s'agit de suspendre leur cycle pour une très courte période.

(*Bluepod* leaflet, 2011)

In this example, *agit* is preceded by *se*, but this *se* cannot be treated as a pronoun. In fact, it simply tells us that the process indicated by the verb does not extend beyond the entity that functions as subject. Genuine reflexivity is simply a special case of this phenomenon. For the moment, for the sake of simplicity, we will consider this item to be part of the verb, or the auxiliary depending on the case.

French also has a number of cases where the verbal group is made up of a finite verb followed by an infinitive, but where it is the infinitive which indicates the process. In the case of the verb *aller*, where *aller* is finite, and the following verb is infinitive, the verb *aller* can be treated as an aspectual auxiliary. In the following example *va . . . suspendre* is a case in point:

(7) On ne va pas suspendre les élections parce qu'il y a une crise.

(*Le Monde*, 13 décembre 2011)

This verbal group can be analysed as follows:

a	v
ne va pas	suspendre

At this stage, the negative adjunct *ne . . . pas* will not an analysed separately.

The modal verbs *vouloir*, *devoir* and *pouvoir* function in the same way. Thus, in the example:

(8) Je veux faire de la CPI une institution aussi humaine que possible, afin qu'elle soit comprise et respectée.

(*Le Monde*, 13 décembre 2011)

The verbal group *veux faire* can be analysed:

a	v
veux	faire

There is a possible alternative to this method of analysis, which involves treating the finite verb as the (main) verb, and not as auxiliary, and the infinitive as the verb of a rankshifted non-finite clause (Banks 2003a). However, we recommend the above analysis for beginning students.

There are a number of other verbs, notably of a mental nature, such as *désirer*, *espérer*, *préférer*, *souhaiter*, which bear a certain similarity to the modal auxiliary verbs, but here the finite verb seems to express a genuine mental process distinct from the meaning of the infinitive, as in the following:

(9) Nous espérons jouer dans cette enceinte dès août 2014.

(*Le Monde*, 13 décembre 2011)

where it seems clear that hoping (*désirons*) and playing (*jouer*) constitute two quite distinct processes. In these cases, the finite verb should be treated as verb, and the infinitive as the verb of a rankshifted clause, here a clause functioning like a noun.

2.3 Prepositional phrases

Finally, we need to deal with prepositional phrases. Prepositional phrases are made up of a preposition followed by a nominal group, which completes the prepositional phrase. Thus, the following example begins with a prepositional phrase:

(10) Dans un bol, mélanger l'oignon au reste de ciboulette et de persil hachés.

(*Femme Actuelle*, 9–15 janvier 2012)

This prepositional phrase begins with the preposition *dans*, which will naturally be called the preposition symbolized by (lower-case) p. The nominal group that follows it will be called the completive, symbolized by (lower-case) c. Thus, the prepositional phrase, *Dans un bol* can be analysed as follows:

p	c
Dans	un bol

If we now return to the example we started with:

(11) Ils ont fêté Noël sur Twitter.

(*Femme Actuelle*, 9–15 janvier 2012)

it is now possible to analyse this in terms of both its groups and its words. The analysis can be presented like this:

S	P	C	A
h Ils	a v ont fêté	h Noël	p c sur Twitter

So, we see that this example has a subject, which is made up of a head, with no modifiers or qualifiers, a predicator, made up of an auxiliary and a verb, a complement, made up of a head, again with no modifiers or qualifiers, and an adjunct made up of a preposition and a completive.

2.4 Rankshift

It may have been noticed that in our treatment of the prepositional phrase *Dans un bol*, we cut a corner. In our analysis, *un bol* is analysed as completive. However, it could be objected that a completive has been defined as a word, but *un bol* is not, strictly speaking, a word, but two words! In other words, it has the structure of a group. So, we might say that in this case *un bol* is a group "pretending" to be a word. *Un bol* has the structure of a group, but functions as a word. We can represent this in our analysis, by refining it as follows:

p	c
	m h
Dans	(un bol)

Groups and words are examples of ranks. We could say that our example *Ils ont fêté Noël sur Twitter* has been analysed at the ranks of group and word. Where an element has the structure of one rank, but functions at a different rank, as in the case of *un bol*, we talk about "rankshift", since the element has shifted or changed from one rank to another. The brackets enclosing *un bol* represent the fact that this segment is rankshifted. In this book, we will deal with three ranks: clause, group, and word.

Consider the following example:

> (12) La victoire de l'Olympique Lyonnais sur la pelouse de Lorient (1–0), dimanche 11 décembre, en match de clôture de la 17e journée de la Ligue 1, conclut une semaine agitée pour le septuple champion de France.
>
> (*Le Monde*, 13 décembre 2011)

The first segment of this example is *La victoire de l'Olympique Lyonnais sur la pelouse de Lorient*. The head of this nominal group is *victoire*, preceded by the definite article as modifier. It is followed by two rankshifted groups functioning as qualifiers: *de l'Olympique Lyonnais*, and *sur la pelouse de Lorient*. The first of these is made up of a preposition and a completive. Since the completive is a proper name, it makes no sense to attempt to analyse it further. The second qualifier is more complex; the preposition, *sur*, is followed by a complex nominal group, *la pelouse de Lorient*, functioning as completive, hence another example of rankshift; this has the head, *pelouse*, preceded by the definite article as modifier, and followed by *de Lorient*, functioning as qualifier; but this itself is a rankshifted group, made up of a preposition and completive. This analysis can be represented as follows:

<table>
<tr><td>m</td><td>h</td><td>q</td><td>q</td></tr>
<tr><td>

La</td><td>

victoire</td><td>p c

(de l'Olympique Lyonnais)</td><td>p c
m h q
p c
(sur (la pelouse (de Lorient)))</td></tr>
</table>

Now consider the following example:

(13) Mitt Romney, qui avait le contrôle de la situation dans les premiers débats, a accumulé les signes de nervosité.

(*Le Monde*, 13 décembre 2011)

Here, the subject is *Mitt Romney, qui avait le contrôle de la situation dans les premiers débats*. The head, *Mitt Romney*, is followed by a relative clause, which gives us more information about the head, so it functions like a qualifier. But its structure is not that of a word, nor even that of a group; its structure is that of a clause (it is after all a relative clause!). This is again an example of rankshift, but in this case the shift is of two places from clause to word, leapfrogging over group, a sort of "double rankshift". Square brackets will be used in the analysis to indicate this type of rankshift of two places. The analysis is as follows:

<table>
<tr><td>h</td><td>q</td></tr>
<tr><td>

Mitt Romney</td><td>S P C
h v m h q
p c
m h

[qui | avait | le contrôle (de (la situation))]</td></tr>
</table>

Since the rankshifted clause has the structure of a clause it must first be analysed in terms of subject, predicator, complement, and adjunct. Here there is a subject, which is made up of a head, *qui*, a predicator, which is made up of the verb, *avait*, and a rather more complex complement. The complement has *contrôle* as head, preceded by the definite article as modifier, and followed by a rankshifted qualifier; this is made up of the preposition *de*, followed by a rankshifted completive, itself made up of the head, *situation*, with the definite article as modifier.

2.5 Analysis of an authentic example

The following is an extract from a piece in the women's magazine *Femme Actuelle*, dated 9–15 janvier 2012.

> Je participe pour la première fois aux NRJ Music Awards, diffusés sur TF1 ! Quand j'ai annoncé à mes filles que j'allais faire cette émission, elles ont sauté de joie. Je suis là pour remettre une récompense à un artiste. Ce n'est pas demain que je vais gagner un NRJ Awards !

<table>
<tr><td>S</td><td>P</td><td>A</td><td>A</td></tr>
<tr><td>h</td><td>v</td><td>p c
m m h</td><td>p c
- h - q
v p c</td></tr>
<tr><td>Je</td><td>participe</td><td>pour (la première fois)</td><td>aux (NRJ Awards [diffusés | sur TF1])</td></tr>
</table>

Since NRJ Awards is a proper noun it has been treated as a single word.

<table>
<tr><td colspan="5">β</td></tr>
<tr><td>A</td><td>S</td><td>P</td><td>A</td><td>C</td></tr>
<tr><td>h</td><td>h</td><td>a v</td><td>p c
m h</td><td>S P C
h a v m h</td></tr>
<tr><td>Quand</td><td>j'</td><td>ai annoncé</td><td>à (mes filles)</td><td>[que j' | allais faire | cette émission]</td></tr>
</table>

<table>
<tr><td colspan="3">α</td></tr>
<tr><td>S</td><td>P</td><td>A</td></tr>
<tr><td>h</td><td>a v</td><td>p c</td></tr>
<tr><td>elles</td><td>ont sauté</td><td>de joie</td></tr>
</table>

This is a clause complex (traditionally called a sentence) made up of two clauses. The first of these is a β-clause. These are subordinate clauses that are not rankshifted to another level. The second is an α-clause. These are main clauses, or coordinate main clauses. The conjunction *quand* tells us about temporal relationships, and so can be treated as an adjunct. The complement in this example is a rankshifted clause. Simple conjunctions, such as *que* in this example, will not be analysed separately here.

<table>
<tr><td>S</td><td>P</td><td>C</td><td>A</td></tr>
<tr><td>h</td><td>v</td><td>h</td><td>p c
v m h p c
m h</td></tr>
<tr><td>Je</td><td>suis</td><td>là</td><td>pour [remettre | une récompense | à (un artiste)]</td></tr>
</table>

<table>
<tr><td>S</td><td>P</td><td>C</td><td>S</td></tr>
<tr><td>h</td><td>v</td><td>h</td><td>S P C
h a v m -h-</td></tr>
<tr><td>Ce</td><td>n'est pas</td><td>demain</td><td>[que je | vais gagner | un NRJ Awards]</td></tr>
</table>

The final clause of this extract is an example of a cleft clause. In this clause, the subject, *ce*, is co-referential with the rankshifted clause, *que je vais gagner un NRJ Awards*. So, in a sense, the subject is expressed twice.

Summary of chapter 2

- Clauses are made up of groups.
- There are four types of group: subject, predicator, complement, and (circumstantial) adjunct.
- Groups are made up of words.
- Some groups, mainly nominal, but also adjectival, have a head, which may be preceded by modifiers, and followed by qualifiers.
- Verbal groups have a verb, which may be preceded by an auxiliary.
- It is possible for the auxiliary to be conjugated, with the verb in the infinitive.
- The so-called reflexive pronoun, *se*, is part of the verb.
- Prepositional phrases are made up of a preposition followed by a completive.
- Rankshift occurs when an element of one rank functions as an element of a different rank.

3 Representing the world

The ideational metafunction

In this chapter, we will see how language is used to represent the external world of physical events and the inner world of our thoughts. We will see that there are different types of process, and each process has a certain number of possible participants. We will also see how these elements can be linked together to form longer stretches of text.

The ideational metafunction, which is a constituent at the semantic level of the systemic model, deals with the representation of the world. It is made up of an experiential function and a logical function. The experiential function concerns the processes, the participants in those processes, and the circumstances in which they occur; the logical function concerns elements that bind these together.

In our version of the systemic model there are five process types. In terms of the grammar, a participant is typically encoded as a nominal group, and hence as subject, complement (direct object), or a non-prepositional indirect object. These are direct partcipants. Participants can appear in prepositional phrases, but in this case they are no longer direct, but indirect participants, and, strictly speaking, are functioning as circumstantial adjuncts. For example, in the following,

> (14) Un peu plus loin, la route est coupée par une énorme barge encore pleine de ciment . . .
>
> (*Le Monde*, 13/14 février 2005)

the *énorme barge* has an agentive role, which can easily be seen if the clause is reformulated in the active voice: *une énorme barge coupe la route*. However, in our example, the *énorme barge* appears in a prepositional phrase. The preposition is the language's way of signalling that the segment is to be read as an adjunct. Hence the phrase *par une énorme barge encore pleine de ciment* expresses an adjunct but an adjunct of an agentive type; that is, it gives us an indirect participant.

We shall now describe each of these process types and their associated participants.

3.1 Material process

The first of these process types, and, in terms of the variety of participant roles that can be associated with it, the most complex, is material process. Material process is a process that takes place in a physical environment; hence it is an action or event of a physical type. In the following clause

(15) M. Chirac se rend à Beyrouth pour signifier son inquiétude.
(headline *Le Monde*, 17 février 2005)

the process encoded by the verb *se rendre* is a material process in that it signifies a movement in space, and hence a movement of a physical nature. With this process a single participant is associated, *M. Chirac*. This is the participant that instigates, or causes, the process to take place. This type of participant is an actor. Hence a partial analysis of this clause would give:

M. Chirac	se rend
Actor	Pro: Mat.

This is the sort of process, traditionally called "intransitive", which, of its nature, has only one participant. In the following clause, however, there are two participants.

(16) Donc, il renoue sa cravate . . .
(*Le Monde*, 17 février 2005)

We are still in the area of material process since *renouer* constitutes a physical action. Moreover, this is the sort of process that naturally involves two participants, an actor that brings about the process, and an affected, the entity that is in some way altered, changed or modified by the process; this type of participant is called the affected. Hence a partial analysis of this clause would give:

il	renoue	sa cravate
Actor	Pro: Mat.	Affected

It is usual for the affected to appear as the second participant, that is, after the verb, when the verb is in the active voice, and as the first and only direct participant if the verb is in the passive voice. In the following clause

> (17) Ce pont a été rajouté pour accueillir les membres d'équipages supplémentaires.
>
> (advertising booklet, 2004)

ce pont is the affected.

Ce pont	a été rajouté
Affected	Pro: Mat.

There are, however, a few verbs that place the affected in subject position even in the active form:

> (18) . . . que le régime de Damas . . . en subira les conséquences.
>
> (*Le Monde*, 17 février 2005)

Here *le régime de Damas* is affected; the second participant, *les conséquences*, has the role of range, which will be dealt with below.

le régime de Damas	subira	les conséquences
Affected	Pro: Mat.	Range

An actor is typically animate, and it is useful to distinguish causal participants that are not animate.

> (19) L'anticyclone situé sur le proche Atlantique dirige sur le pays un flux du nord.
>
> (*Le Monde*, 17 février 2005)

In this clause, the participant that causes the process to take place is *l'anticyclone situé sur le proche Atlantique*. Although this is the causal entity that brings about the process *diriger*, it is not an animate, conscious entity but a natural force. We use the term force for this type of participant.

L'anticyclone situé sur le proche Atlantique	dirige	un flux du nord
Force	Pro: Mat.	Affected

There are also inanimate participants that can have a causal role in a process, but that, like the key that opens a door, do not act of themselves but require an animate conscious agent in order to do so. We call this type of participant an instrument. The conscious agent will usually be implicit, and hence not mentioned directly in the clause. Thus, in the following:

(20) . . . une attaque contre des boulangeries chiites a fait sept tués.
(*Le Monde*, 13/14 février 2005)

The *attaque* is what killed the seven people, but the *attaque* does not take place without there being agents who are using the *attaque* as a means of achieving some end. Hence the analysis is as follows:

une attaque contre des boulangeries chiites	a fait	sept tués
Instrument	Pro: Mat.	Affected

In some cases, one of the participants is created by the process. This must be distinguished from the affected, which exists before the process takes place but is changed by it. A participant that is created by the process is known as a result.

(21) . . . nous avons créé Ricochet, un journal de ville, à Orsay (91).
(*Le Télégramme*, 21 mars 2007)

Here, *Ricochet, un journal de ville* did not exist before the process of creation, and so is a result.

nous	avons créé	Ricochet, un journal de ville
Actor	Pro: Mat.	Result

There is a further case where a participant, typically the second participant, is not an affected, since it is not changed or modified by the process, but simply gives the extent of the process; this will frequently give the place where the process takes place, but it is encoded as a direct participant, as in *cross the street*, or *climb the stairs* in English. This is called a range.

(22) Le navigateur Guy Bernardin, 62 ans, a bouclé hier matin, en Nouvelle-Zélande, la deuxième étape de son tour du monde en solitaire . . .
(*Le Télégramme*, 22 mars 2007)

In this example, *la deuxième étape* does not change because it has been completed; it simply gives the route that has been covered.

Le navigateur Guy Bernadin, 62 ans	a bouclé	la deuxième étape de son tour du monde en solitaire
Actor	Pro: Mat.	Range

The concept of range includes two sub-types. The one we have just introduced is an entity range. In other cases, the range repeats, frequently in some modified or more precise form, the process itself.

(23) Au fil des étés, elle prend l'habitude de rédiger des carnets de voyage.

(*TV Magazine*, 18 février 2007)

The verb *prendre* tells us very little about the process going on. It is the complement (*l'habitude de rédiger . . .*) which tells us what is really happening. Thus, the content of the process has been largely transferred to the complement. This too is a range, but of the sub-type we call a process range.

elle	prend	l'habitude de rédiger des carnets de voyage
Actor	Pro: Mat.	Range

There remain two participant roles that can occur in material process. These are in fact very similar, and they only occur in processes that can have three participants. One of these is the participant towards whom the process is directed, called the receiver; and the other is the participant for whom the process is carried out, called the beneficiary.

(24) . . . les résidants peuvent vendre leur logement, notamment en viager, ce qui leur assure une rente à vie, indexée sur l'inflation.

(*Le Monde*, 13/14 février 2005)

In this example *leur* is the participant towards whom the process is directed in the sense that they receive the *rente*, it comes to them.

ce qui	leur	assure	une rente à vie, indexée sur l'inflation
Instrument	Receiver	Pro: Mat.	Affected

It should be noticed that, in French, only a pronoun can function as receiver. A noun or nominal group can only function as an indirect receiver. Thus, in the following, *à un photographe majeur et mal traité chez nous* functions grammatically as an adjunct and hence as an indirect receiver.

(25) Le jeu de paume, à Paris, rend hommage à un photographe majeur et mal traité chez nous . . .

(*Le Monde*, 29/30 août 2010)

Here, *Le jeu de paume* is understood as the people running that institution, and thus functions as actor in a material process.

Le jeu de paume, à Paris	rend	hommage	à un photographe majeur et mal traité chez nous . . .
Actor	Pro: Mat	Range	Circs: indirect receiver

French, unlike English, can have a receiver whose direction is negative, that is, the process is directed away from rather than towards this participant.

(26) . . . onze familles de Cachan (Val-de-Marne) ont accepté que leur poste de télévision leur soit retiré . . .

(*Le Monde Télévision*, 13/14 février 2005)

Thus, the television set is taken away from these families. We will continue to use the same role label for these, so that receiver covers those cases where the process is directed towards or away from the participant.

leur poste de télévision	leur	soit retiré
Affected	Receiver	Pro: Mat.

In English, it is usual to distinguish between a receiver and a beneficiary, the former being the participant towards whom the process is directed and the latter the participant on behalf of whom the process is carried out. These can be readily distinguished by producing the prepositional variants, where the participants are indirect and encoded as adjuncts. The receiver has the preposition *to*, and the beneficiary, the preposition *for*. This preposition probe is obviously not valid for French, and in any case the participant roles of receiver and beneficiary are relatively minor in French to the extent that they can only be encoded by pronouns. Encoding with a noun requires that the participant be introduced by a preposition, and hence the participant can only be indirect, and encoded as an adjunct. Hence for practical purposes the receiver can be extended to cover both of these types of participant, except where a high degree of delicacy is required.

3.2 Mental process

In comparison, mental process is relatively simple in terms of the participant roles associated with it. A mental process is one that takes place in a cerebral environment. It has three basic sub-types: cognitive, perceptive, and affective. Cognitive mental processes are processes of thinking; perceptive mental processes are processes of sensing, whether they be motivated (*écouter, regarder* . . .) or not (*entendre, voir* . . .); and affective mental processes are processes of liking and disliking. A mental process, of its nature, requires a conscious participant who is the cerebral site of the mental process. This participant is called the senser. Clauses of mental process usually also express the content of the experience. This is called the phenomenon. The following is an example of a cognitive mental process:

(27) Elle-même sait que, si elle avait été juste jolie, voilà bien longtemps que les critiques ne l'auraient pas ratée.

(*TV Magazine*, 18 février 2007)

The following is an example of perceptive mental process:

(28) Je ne regarde jamais un film en entier.

(*TV Magazine*, 18 février 2007)

And an example of affective mental process is to be found in the subordinate clause of this example:

(29) J'y trouve tout ce que j'aime. . . .

(*Le Monde Télévision*, 13/14 février 2005)

All of these can be analysed in terms of senser and phenomenon.

Elle-même	sait	que, si elle avait été juste jolie, voilà bien longtemps que les critiques ne l'aurait pas ratée.
Senser	Pro: Ment.	Phenomenon

Je	ne regarde	un film
Senser	Pro: Ment.	Phenomenon

ce que	j'	aime
Phenomenon	Senser	Pro: Ment.

As is the case in the first of these, rankshifted clauses frequently function as phenomenon.

3.3 Relational process

In a relational process, a relationship is stated either between two entities or between an entity and one of its properties. This may give the impression that relational process is purely static. This is generally the case, but there is an exception to this: processes of becoming. Since processes of becoming express the coming into existence of a state, they are assimilated to relational processes, but they are to some extent themselves dynamic. There are three sub-types of relational process. The first of these is the attributive type. In this type a relationship is set up between an entity and one of its properties. It is therefore descriptive in nature.

(30) Les coquillages que vous pêchez sont des organismes filtreurs qui peuvent concentrer des bactéries pathogènes ou des algues toxiques.

(tourist leaflet, 2004)

This type links an entity, the carrier, with one of its properties, the attribute. The attribute can have the form of a noun group, usually indefinite (as here), or of an adjectival group, or of a prepositional phrase. In this last case, the prepositional phrase situates the carrier and can be thought of as a temporary property.

Les coquillages que vous pêchez	sont	des organismes filtreurs qui peuvent concentrer des bactéries pathogènes ou des algues toxiques
Carrrier	Pro: Rel.	Attribute

The following is an example of the becoming type:

(31) Générale des Eaux est devenue l'un des meilleurs spécialistes des métiers d'eaux dans le monde entier.

(circular letter, c.2006)

Générale des Eaux	est devenue	l'un des meilleurs spécialistes des métiers d'eaux dans le monde entier
Carrier	Pro: Rel.	Attribute

The second sub-type is the identifying relational process. In this case the two participants are co-referential, but one of them serves to identify the other. The entity that is identified is the token, and the entity used to identify it is the value.

(32) La cabine juste à l'extérieur du carré est celle de Solander, un naturaliste suédois, tuteur et ami de Joseph Banks.

(tourist leaflet, 2004)

Thus, the cabin is identified as being Solander's cabin. The relationship is an exclusive one, unlike the attributive type, where the attribute may be applied to entities other than the carrier.

La cabine juste à l'extérieur du carré	est	celle de Solander, un naturaliste suédois, tuteur et ami de Joseph Banks
Token	Pro: Rel.	Value

It is frequently said that the token and value can be inverted, while the carrier and attribute cannot. This is not strictly true. In the case of identifying process, the value can quite easily take up subject position, and the token complement position; in the case of attributive process, the attribute can appear in subject position but this is fairly rare and usually requires a specific genre, for example, poetry.

The third type of relational process is that of possessive relational process, which links a possessor and a possessed. This includes not only cases of possession, properly so-called, but also other situations, such as inclusion, which might be thought of as a form of abstract possession.

(33) Rennes a son prix Goncourt, désormais presque aussi célèbre que son aîné.

(tourist booklet, 2002)

Rennes	a	son prix Goncourt, désormais presque aussi célèbre que son aîné
Possessor	Pro: Rel.	Possessed

The following is an example of the more abstract type:

(34) Les articles . . . comprendront une présentation de l'auteur . . .

(circular letter, 2007)

Les articles	comprendront	une présentation de l'auteur
Possessor	Pro: Rel.	Possessed

3.4 Verbal process

Verbal processes are processes of communication. Some linguists restrict verbal processes to those that can project, that is, that can have as a complement a section of direct or indirect speech (Caffarel 2006). We feel that it is more appropriate to have a purely semantic definition of process types, and so we will include within the category of verbal process all processes that express a form of linguistic communication, whether it be written or spoken. Verbal process typically involves two participants, the entity performing the communication, and the content of the communication.

> (35) François Bayrou a exposé, hier, ses propositions concernant les retraites . . .
>
> (*Le Télégramme*, 21 mars 2007)

In this example, there is a person who communicates, *François Bayrou*, and this type of participant is called the sayer, and the content of his message, *ses propositions concernant les retraites*, is called the verbiage.

François Bayrou	a exposé	ses propositions concernant les retraites
Sayer	Pro: Verb.	Verbiage

It is also possible for the addressee to appear as a third participant.

> (36) . . . .la scripte m'a confié que j'étais le rayon de soleil de l'équipe.
>
> (*Le Télégramme*, 18 février 2007)

Since the addressee is the person towards whom the process is directed, we can here consider this to be the same function that was found in material process, that of receiver.

la scripte	m'	a confié	que j'étais le rayon de soleil de l'équipe
Sayer	Receiver	Pro: Verb.	Verbiage

Sometimes, rather than the person communicating, the document itself is given as a sort of substitute sayer.

> (37) Le livre décrit les espoirs et les désillusions de Ferenc Kolyeszar, policier et écrivain qui déchante en enquêtant sur la mort de la femme d'un membre du Parti . . .
>
> (*Le Monde*, 18 février 2007)

In this case, it is not the *livre* that is strictly doing the communicating, but the author who is communicating through his book. The book is therefore the means of communication, and it seems more appropriate to analyse this, as in material process, as an instrument.

Le livre	décrit	les espoirs et les désillusions de Ferenc Kolyeszar, policier et écrivain qui déchante en enquêtant sur la mort de la femme d'un membre du Parti
Instrument	Pro: verb.	Verbiage

3.5 Existential process

Finally, there is a small process type, where the proposition simply states the existence of some entity. In French, this is frequently done using the expression *il y a.*

(38) Aujourd'hui, il y a environ 70.000 Français vivant à New York.
(*Le Télégramme*, 29 octobre 2011)

In this type of process there is a single participant, that which is said to exist, and this is the existent. The item that functions grammatically as subject, *il*, has no referent and so has no semantic content; consequently it has no participant role.

il	y a	environ 70.000 Français vivant à New York
	Pro: Exist.	Existent

From a purely formal point of view, the sequence *y a* could be said to be made up of a pronoun and a verb, but in present-day French the sequence is indissociable, and it is reasonable to consider this to be a complex verb. Also fairly common, but less so than *il y a*, is the verb *exister*; this is also often used with an expletive, or non-referential, *il* subject.

(39) Effectivement, il existe des familles à risque d'accident cardio-vasculaire.
(*Bien-être et Santé*, février 2007)

Here again, *il* has no participant role, and *des familles à risque d'accident cardiovasculaire* is the existent.

il	existe	des familles à risque d'accident cardiovasculaire
	Pro: Exist.	Existent

However, other ways of expressing existential process do exist.

> (40) D'une performance, il ne reste que la réminiscence affaiblie et organisée.
>
> (*Le Monde*, 19 février 2005)

This clause states that *la reminiscence affaiblie et organisée* is the only thing that still exists.

il	ne reste que	la reminiscence affaiblie et organisée
	Pro: Exist.	Existent

3.6 Finite modal verbs

French differs from English in having modal verbs that are conjugated. The question then arises as to how clauses containing these verbs are to be treated.

> (41) Je pouvais passer des journées sans rien manger . . .
>
> (*Elle*, 20 juillet 2007)

There would seem to be two possible ways to analyse clauses of this type. The first is more analytical, the second more global. The analytical analysis treats *pouvais* as the finite verb, with the non-finite infinitive clause, *passer des journées sans rien manger*, as its complement.

Je	pouvais	passer des journées sans rien manger
Subject	Predicator	Complement

The alternative, more global, point of view is to treat *pouvais passer* as a verbal complex, on the analogy of what is sometimes called phase.

Je	pouvais passer	des journées	sans rien manger
Subject	Predicator	Complement	Adjunct

This makes the transitivity analysis relatively simple.

Je	pouvais passer	des journées	sans rien manger
Actor	Pro: Mat.	Range	Circ: manner

However, this at least leaves open the suspicion that the clause is being treated from an English-centred perspective, and that the French verbal group is being treated in the same way as the equivalent verbal group in English. But in English the modal element is not conjugated, and hence is not finite, and can only be auxiliary to the following (conjugated) verb. In English, there can be no question of treating the modal verb as a carrier of transitivity. But in French this is quite possible. This is the more analytical approach. Nevertheless, this raises a serious problem: if *pouvais*, in the above clause is to be analysed for transitivity, then what type of process is it? One easy way out would be to say that French has a process type that does not exist in English, namely, modal process. This seems, however, to be dodging the issue. It has been suggested (Banks 2003a) that the finite modal verbs of French should be treated as a type of relational process. This seems reasonable in the light of the above example where the subject, *je*, stands in a (modal) relationship to the infinitive clause, which functions as complement. As is frequently the case with more abstract examples, this can be construed either in terms of attribution or of possession.

Je	pouvais	passer des journées sans rien manger
Carrier	Pro: Rel.	Attribute
Possessor		Possessed

Hence there seem to be two possible ways of analysing these clauses, and we would not wish to categorically exclude either of them, believing that a certain degree of relativity is probably endemic in language (Banks 2003b). Nevertheless, for beginning students treating these cases as complex verbal groups is probably simpler, and more intuitively satisfying.

3.7 Analysis of an authentic example

The following is an extract from the introduction of a tourist brochure for the French department of Finistère (c.2005).

> Sur les bords de l'Aven, Gauguin déploie son chevalet. Amoureux solitaire, Prévert déambule la rue de Siam. Au large, le dundee d'un Johnny de Roscoff croise le sillage d'un géant des mers des temps modernes. En baie de Douarnenez, les flots se retirent mais Ys est définitivement engloutie. Merlin et Viviane s'échangent de doux secrets à l'orée d'une forêt enchantée, un menhir fièrement dressé salue le jour naissant, un druide s'éclipse furtivement. Stivell égrène les sons cristallins d'une harpe celtique. Denez clame un kan an diskan, et partout, des Montagne Noires à l'Aber Wrac'h, de la Pointe du Raz à la Baie de Molaix, le Finistère vit, chante et danse, accorde ses pas au rythme des sonneurs et parade majestueusement dans une féerie de couleurs . . .

The following is a suggested analysis of the processes and related participants in this text. Even on a discursive reading, it is evident that that is an attempt to give a highly romanticized image of the region; this poses some problems for the analysis of the text, which will be discussed as we go along.

Gauguin	déploie	son chevalet
Actor	Pro: Mat	Affected

The first clause seems quite straightforward, with a material process accompanied by an actor, as first participant, in subject position, and an affected, as second participant, in complement position.

Amoureux solitaire, Prévert	déambule	la rue de Siam
Actor	Pro: Mat	Range

The second clause seems equally straightforward. The only difference here is that the item that functions as grammatical complement is not an affected; it localizes the process and hence is a range.

le dundee d'un Johnny de Roscoff	croise	le sillage d'un géant des mers des temps modernes
Instrument	Pro: Mat	Range

In the third clause, the causal item is not a conscious being, but does require a conscious being, here unmentioned, in order to act. Hence it is analysed as instrument. The second participant is again one that localizes the action, and is hence a range.

les flots	se retirent
Force	Pro: Mat

Here there is a single participant. It is not a conscious entity, but it does act without the intervention of a conscious entity; hence it is a force. The so-called "reflexive pronoun" does not constitute a second participant. In fact, strictly speaking, it is not really a pronoun, but a part of the verbal group indicating that the process is intensive, as opposed to extensive, that is, it has no effect beyond the first participant itself (Banks 2009a, 2010a).

Ys	est . . . engloutie
Affecté	Pro: Mat

With clauses of this type, analysts frequently hesitate between treating the clause as passive or as relational, that is, in the present case, between treating *engloutie* as the past participle in a passive verb, or as an adjective. This is fairly natural, since the passive, of its very nature, has a static feel about it. We take the option of analysing all forms of *être* + past participle as passive, unless it is impossible to do so. Hence, in this clause, the verb is treated as being the passive of *engloutir*. The only participant is affected, and the supposed causal force, the sea, is unmentioned. Both these features occur in most passive clauses.

Merlin et Viviane	s'échangent	de doux secrets
Sayer	Pro: Verb	Verbiage

Here we have the first example in this text of a clause that is not material process. This is a question of communication and hence a verbal process. It will be noted that the process is of a reciprocal type, in that Merlin and Viviane are both communicating, but at the same time receiving the communication of the other.

The next clause, *un menhir . . . salue le jour naissant*, is the most difficult we have seen so far in this text. This is partly because the clause is obviously a metaphor. If we take the metaphor at face value, then we have one entity hailing another. This involves a further difficulty, since the process can be conceived of as verbal, "saying hello", or as material, "waving your hand". In the first case this would give:

un menhir	salue	le jour naissant
Sayer	Pro: Verb	Receiver

The second option would give:

un menhir	salue	le jour naissant
Actor	Pro: Mat	Range

However, it is evident that a menhir cannot be a sayer or an actor except in a metaphorical sense, nor can the dawn be the receiver of a message. It is precisely this that is the essential part of the metaphor. If we ask ourselves what is really happening, then we would have to say, nothing much: the menhir is simply there at the break of day. This would suggest that a literal reading of the clause would give us an existential process, with *le jour naissant* as an adjunct of time:

un menhir	salue
Existent	Pro: Exist

However, none of these analyses individually give a satisfactory interpretation of the clause, and we probably need a conflation of all three to obtain something like an acceptable analysis:

un menhir	salue	le jour naissant
Sayer/Actor	Pro: Verb/Mat	Receiver/Range
Existent	Pro: Exist	

With the next clause, we return to something more straightforward:

un druide	s'éclipse
Actor	Pro: Mat

This clause has a single participant as actor with a material process, encoded by a verb with the intenstifying particle *se*.

Stivell	égrène	les sons cristallins
Actor	Pro: Mat	Range

Some might feel that *les sons cristallins* is the result, but it has been analysed here as range since it is part of the process itself.

Denez	clame	un kan an diskan
Actor	Pro: Mat	Range

In this analysis, singing an unaccompanied folksong is considered as a physical act. Some might feel that this is in some sense communicating a message, in which case this would give the following alternative analysis:

Denez	clame	un kan an diskan
Sayer	Pro: Verb	Verbiage

Finally, we come to the last clause complex of the extract, which has a series of verbs, all of which can be analysed as material. The first three have a single participant, which is only mentioned once:

le Finistère	vit
Actor	Pro: Mat

(le Finistère)	chante
(Actor)	Pro: Mat

(le Finistère)	danse
(Actor)	Pro: Mat

The last process has two participants:

(le Finistère)	accorde	ses pas
(Actor)	Pro: Mat	Range

Here, *le Finistère* can be taken either in the sense of the people of the region, or, metaphorically, as the region itself.

This extract is predominantly material in terms of the processes involved, and thus gives an image of a region imbued with physical activity. At the same time the actors involved are mainly historical or mythical figures, and this combined with a good dose of metaphor, produces a romantic picture of the area, which is presumably the intention of those who wrote this piece.

3.8 The logical function

The logical function, mentioned at the beginning of this chapter, deals with the ways units are linked together. The basic distinction is between units of equal status, called parataxis, and between units of different status, called hypotaxis. At the level of the clause, clauses that are in a coordinate relationship would be said to be paratactic.

> (42) L'ancien jeune ministre se revendique d'une droite moderne, mais clame depuis des mois son opposition à la primaire.
>
> (*Le Nouvel Observateur*, 12 décembre 2013)

In this clause complex, there are two clauses linked by the coordinator *mais*. There is no hierarchical relationship between these clauses: they are of equal status, so this is an example of parataxis.

> (43) Si j'étais pris en entrant à Soweto, je pouvais être arrêté.
>
> (*Le Nouvel Observateur*, 12 décembre 2013)

In this clause complex, the first clause expresses the condition for the second. The first clause could not stand on its own; it is dependent on the second, hence this is an example of hypotaxis.

Both paratactic and hypotactic relationships can be divided into two basic types: expansion and projection. Expansion is where the dependant clause elaborates, extends or enhances the main clause.

In elaboration, one clause gives more information about another, by restatement, clarification, or exemplification.

> (44) Hachemi Rafsandjani est recalé par le conseil des gardiens de la constitution : il ne pourra pas briguer la présidence.
>
> (*Marianne*, 25–31 mai 2013)

In this example the second clause elaborates on the first by clarifying the intended meaning of *recalé*.

In extension, one clause expands another by giving extra information, or suggests an exception or alternative.

> (45) Mais nombre de Français aimerait que les personnes dangereuses ne soient jamais libérées, et le terrorisme aggrave cette humeur mauvaise.
>
> (*Ouest France*, 9 août 2016)

In this case the second clause adds an additional point to what has been said in the first clause.

Enhancement occurs when one clause embellishes another by qualifying it in some way; this includes circumstantial qualification of time, place, cause, and condition.

> (46) Et quand, le 3 août, les Kurdes irakiens ont fui devant les attaques de l'Etat islamique dans le district de Sinjar, c'est la branche syrienne du PKK qui s'est interpose – le massif du Sinjar est à 20 kilomètres du Kurdistan syrien.
>
> (*Le Nouvel Observateur*, 21 août 2014)

The first clause is a temporal clause, and thus gives a circumstanial embellishment to the second clause.

Projection is the relationship whereby we express words or thoughts, and thus corresponds to what has frequently been called direct or indirect speech or thought. Where it is a question of speech, whether it be direct or indirect, it is a case of locution.

> (47) "On ne vit qu'une fois", se justifie-t-il.
>
> (*Ouest France*, 9 août 2016)

In this example of locution, we have a quote of the exact words. In the following the sense of the words is given without quoting the exact words.

(48) Ils lui demande si elle voudra bien faire le guet.

(*Femina*, 22–28 septembre 2014)

In the following example, it is not words that are represented but thoughts.

(49) Benoît voulait que Sophie soit très sensible, qu'elle ait une forme d'inquiétude permanente.

(*Femina*, 22–28 septembre 2014)

This is a case or idea, rather than location.

Summary of chapter 3

- The ideational metafunction consists of the experiential function and the logical function.
- The experiential function concerns processes, participants, and, if there are any, the circumstances.
- There are five process types: material, mental, relational, verbal, and existential.
- Material processes are events or actions of a physical nature.
- Mental processes are events of a cerebral type.
- Relational processes state a relationship between two entities or between an entity and one of its characteristics.
- Verbal processes are processes of communication.
- Existential processes state the existence of an entity.
- The following are the possible participants in a material process:

  Actor: the conscious instigator of the process.
  Force: the non-conscious cause of the process.
  Instrument: a non-conscious cause where there is a supposed conscious agent.
  Affected: the entity modified by the process.
  Range: the extent, or extension, of the process.
  Result: the entity created by the process.
  Receiver: the entity to whom, or for whom, the process is carried out.

- There are two possible participants in a mental process:

  Senser: the conscious entity who experiences the mental process.
  Phenomenon: the content of the mental experience.

- The participants in a relational process depend on the process sub type:
  In attributive relational process:

  Carrier: the entity of which something is attributed.
  Attributed: the feature that is attributed.

In identifying relational process:

Token: the entity that is being identified.
Value: the item with which the token is identified.

In possessive relational process:

Possessor: the entity that is said to possess something.
Possessed: the entity that is the possession.

- The following are the possible participants in a verbal process:

Sayer: the person who is communicating.
Verbiage: the content of the message communicated.
Receiver: the person to whom the message is addressed.
Instrument: the entity used to convey the message.

- Existential processes have only one participant: the existent, which is the entity said to exist.
- The logical function deals with the ways in which units are linked together.
- Parataxis is the linking of units of equal status.
- Hypotaxis is the linking of units of unequal status.
- Clauses can be extended by expansion or projection.
- Expansion can be done through elaboration, extension, or enhancement.

Elaboration restates, clarifies, or exemplifies the clause.
Extension provides extra information or gives exceptions or alternatives.
Enhancement embellishes with qualifications or circumstances.

- Projection gives the content of speech, a locution, or thought, an idea.

4 Creating relationships

The interpersonal metafunction

In this chapter, we will see how a speaker establishes a relationship with those with whom he is communicating, and how he relates to the content of his message. We will also see the types of acts that speech involves.

The interpersonal metafunction deals with relationships. These are relationships established by the speaker, either with his addressees, or with the message he is communicating.

4.1 Mood

As it has been developed for English (Halliday 2014, Banks 2005), the interpersonal metafunction distinguishes between a mood element, mood for short, and the residue. The main constituents of the mood are the finite and the subject, so that in an English clause such as:

(50) A powerful group of News Corp shareholders have accused Rupert Murdoch of "egregious" behaviour . . .

(*Guardian Weekly*, 15–21 juillet 2011)

the mood structure of the interpersonal metafunction can be analysed as follows:

A powerful group of News Corp shareholders have	accused Rupert Murdoch of "egrarious" behaviour . . .
Mood	Residue

This is seen most clearly in the formation of interrogative mood, where the relative positions of subject and finite are inversed while the rest of the clause remains the same.

Have a powerful group of News Corp shareholders	accused Rupert Murdoch of "egrarious" behaviour . . . ?
Mood	Residue

Polar questions in French function in exactly the same way when the subject is a pronoun, as in:

(51) Avez-vous accepté facilement de devoir vous vieillir pour ce rôle ?
(*Bien-être et Santé*, février 2007)

This would give the following analysis:

Avez-vous	accepté facilement de devoir vous vieillir pour ce rôle ?
Mood	Residue

Where, however, the subject is a noun group, this is placed in initial position, and is repeated in pronominal form in the post-finite interrogative position:

(52) La France a-t-elle pour autant perdu totalement la bataille de l'éolien ?
(*Le Monde*, 27 août 2010)

This would then be analyzed:

La France a-t-elle	pour autant perdu totalement la bataille de l'éolien ?
Mood	Residue

French has no default auxiliary comparable to *do* in English. Consequently, in French, where there is no auxiliary, and the finite is consequently fused with the verb, the interrogative is formed by inverting the subject and verb where the subject is a pronoun, and where the subject is a noun group, by placing this in initial position, and repeating it in pronominal form after the verb. In these cases, it is that part of the predicator that corresponds to the finite plus the subject that constitute the mood element. The following is an example with a pronominal subject:

(53) Imaginez-vous avoir recours un jour à la chirurgie ésthétique ?
(*Version Femina*, 18–24 juillet 2011)

This can be analysed as follows:

<table>
<tr><td colspan="2">Imaginez-vous</td><td>avoir recours un jour à la chirurgie ésthétique ?</td></tr>
<tr><td>Res-</td><td>Mood</td><td>-idue</td></tr>
</table>

The following is an example with a nominal subject.

(54) . . . le peuple que j'ai vu tellement présent et attentif au cours des ces années va-t-elle venir vers nous . . . ?

(Ségolène Royal, *Primaires Socialistes*, 2011)

. . . le peuple que j'ai vu tellement présent et attentif au cours des ces années va-t-		elle	venir vers nous . . . ?
Mo-	Res-	-od	-idue

In addition, French has an interrogative marker, *Est-ce que*. This is placed initially in a clause that otherwise has the same structure as an affirmative clause. In these cases, the interrogative marker plus the subject and finite, or fused finite and verb, constitute the mood element:

(55) Est-ce qu'elle vous ressemble un peu ?

(*Version Femina*, 18–24 juillet 2011)

This can be analysed as follows:

Est-ce qu'elle vous ressemble		un peu ?
Mood	Residue	

Alice Caffarel takes a different point of view on this question (Caffarel 2004, 2006). She argues that in French the mood structure should be analysed in terms of a negotiator and a remainder, where the negotiator is composed of the subject, the finite, and the predicator. This means that the first three of the above examples would, in Caffarel's approach, be analysed as follows:

Avez-vous accepté	facilement de devoir vous vieillir pour ce rôle ?
Negotiator	Remainder

La France a-t-elle pour autant perdu	totalement la bataille de l'éolien ?
Negotiator	Remainder

Imaginez-vous avoir	recours un jour à la chirurgie ésthétique ?
Negotiator	Remainder

This has something to be said for it. As Caffarel points out, the interpersonal function is a question of communicative exchange, and this is a negotiation that involves subject, finite, and predicator. However, she believes that this is a specificity of French that distinguishes it from English. On the other hand, English clauses seem perfectly amenable to this treatment. The English clause above could be analysed:

A powerful group of News Corp shareholders have accused	Rupert Murdoch of "egrarious" behaviour . . .
Negotiator	Remainder

Hence we believe that the negotiator–remainder analysis of the mood structure is not a specifically French phenomenon, but simply a different way of looking at the interpersonal metafunction (Banks 2010b).

4.2 Analysis of an authentic example

The following is an extract from the French regional newspaper, *Le Télégramme*, for 29 October 2011.

> Alors qu'au début de l'enquête Hicheim Gharallah, 34 ans, niait les faits, au cours de l'audience, il a reconnu avoir sciemment transmis le VIH à son ancienne compagne et avoir eu des rapports sexuels non protégés avec deux autres jeunes femmes, qui n'ont pas été contaminées. Avant que la cour ne parte délibérer, il leur a demandé "pardon", les yeux dans les yeux. Tout en se défendant de vouloir "faire du Zola", l'avocat de l'accusé, Me Pascal Garbarini, a lui dressé le portait d'un homme mal aimé. "Certes, il a fait du mal", mais c'est un homme en souffrance", a-t-il dit. "On a criminalisé" des faits, mais est-ce qu'on a prévu des soins, un suivi ?".

The first line in the following analyses gives our analysis, the second line gives the analysis according to Caffarel's principles.

<table>
<tr><td>au début de l'enquête</td><td colspan="2">Hicheim Gharammah, 34 ans niait</td><td>les faits</td></tr>
<tr><td>Res-</td><td>Mood</td><td colspan="2">-idue</td></tr>
<tr><td>Re-</td><td colspan="2">Negotiator</td><td>-mainder</td></tr>
</table>

au cours de l'audience	il a	reconnu	avoir sciemment transmis le VIH à son ancienne compagne et avoir eu des rapports sexuels non protégés avec deux autres jeunes femmes, qui n'ont pas été contaminées.
Res-	Mood	-idue	
Re-	Negotiator		-mainder

qui n'ont pas été contaminées.	
Mood	Residue
Negotiator	

Since this clause is made up of subject, finite, predicator, the three elements that constitute Caffarel's negotiator, the clause is entirely negotiator and there is no remainder.

la cour ne parte délibérer	
Mood	Residue
Negotiator	Remainder

Il	leur	a	demandé « pardon », les yeux dans les yeux
Mo-	Res-	-od	-idue
Negotiator			Remainder

Caffarel counts pre-finite pronouns as part of the negotiator, on the grounds that they are clitics.

l'avocat de l'accusé, Me Pascal Gabarini a, lui, dressé le portrait d'un homme mal aimé	
Mood	Residue
Negotiator	Remainder

il a	fait	du mal
Mood	Residue	
Negotiator		Remainder

c' est un homme en souffrance	
Mood	Residue
Negotiator	Remainder

« c'est un homme en souffrance », a-t-il dit.		
Res-	Mood	-idue
Remainder	Negotiator	

On a criminalisé des faits	
Mood	Residue
Negotiator	Remainder

est-ce qu'on a prévu des soins, un suivi ?		
Mood		Residue
M-int	Negotiator	Residue

In questions containing the *est-ce que* marker, Caffarel calls this the mood interrogator (M-int), and considers it, strictly speaking, to be outside of the mood structure (Caffarel 2006).

4.3 Modality

Modality is a linguistic resource whereby the speaker comments on the ideational content of his clause, claiming, rather than stating it as a fact, that it is possible, permissible, obligatory, etc. Among the modals, it is possible to distinguish those that are epistemic, that is relating to the speaker's state of knowledge, thus expressing possibility, probability, and certainty. In systemic functional terminology, this is frequently referred to as modalization. Those that are not epistemic are referred to as root modals, and these can be further divided into those that are dynamic and those that are deontic. This is often called modulation in systemic terminology. Dynamic modality relates to the physical world, and thus expresses notions like ability, and physical possibility. Deontic modality relates to the moral world, and expresses permission and obligation.

As was mentioned above, French can express modality by the use of "auxiliaries", which in fact are finite and followed by an infinitive. Rowlett (2007) calls these "pseudo-modals". There are two verbs of this type: *pouvoir*, expressing ability or possibility, which can thus encode both epistemic and root modality, and *devoir*, expressing obligation or necessity, so again, capable of expressing both epistemic and root modality. Some would add to this *vouloir*, which functions in the same way and expresses willingness.

In the following example the verb *pouvoir* (*on peut*) is followed by the passive infinitive *être happé*:

(56) Même isolé dans un village comme Nérac (Lot-et-Garonne), on peut être happé par des rêves de bohème électrique.

(*Le Monde*, 16 novembre 2012)

In the following example the verb *devoir* (*nous devons*) is followed by the infinitive *restaurer*:

(57) Pour repartir à la conquête de notre compétitivité perdue, nous devons restaurer notre compétitivité-coût au travers d'un allégement de la fiscalité qui pèse sur le travail (TVA social).

(*Le Monde*, 16 novembre 2012)

Although some would add *vouloir* to this group of "auxiliaires", it is doubtful whether this is justified. While it is true that *vouloir* can be followed by an infinitive, and in such clauses then looks formally similar to *pouvoir* and *devoir*, the verb *vouloir* in such cases can be analysed as a main verb encoding mental process, with the following non-finite infinitive clause as phenomenon.

(58) C'est pour aider à ce développement que nous voulons élargir notre capital.

(*Nouvel Observateur*, 12 décembre 2013)

In this example, *voulons* functions as a mental process, and *élargir notre capital* is its phenomenon.

French also has the verb *falloir*, which is impersonal, that is, it only functions with a non-referential pronoun, *il*, as subject.

(59) Pour décrocher un tel crédit dans sa banque, il faudra donc faire preuve de persévérance.

(*Mieux Vivre Votre Argent*, mars 2014)

The verb *pouvoir* also turns up in the impersonal expression *il se peut que*.

(60) Il se peut que des pirates soient en train d'essayer de dérober vos informations sur le site hotmail.fr . . .

(commentcamarche.net, 8 décembre 2014)

French occasionally also uses adverbs, adjectives and nouns to express modality. In the following example, modality is expressed through the adverb *peut-être.*

> (61) Peut-être espéraient-ils aussi se saisir de l'évangéliste occidental légèrement exalté, qui vient de temps en temps dans la région promouvoir sa version du salut.
>
> (*Le Monde*, 16 novembre 2012)

In the following example, it is the adjective *obligatoire* that expresses modality.

> (62) Première chose, la scolarisation des enfants n'est obligatoire qu'à partir de 6 ans.
>
> (*Version Femina*, 21 septembre 2014)

And in this example, modality is expressed by using the noun *possibilité.*

> (63) C'est une possibilité parmi d'autres, mais une possibilité sérieuse qu'il a évoquée avec ses proches et quelques ténors de l'UMP.
>
> (*Nouvel Observateur*, 12 décembre 2013)

Adjectives also occur in the form of extraposed structures.

> (64) Ici, il est possible de déduire la totalité des intérêts des revenus fonciers.
>
> (*Mieux Vivre Votre Argent*, mars 2014)

Finally, French has a number of lexical verbs which can be used to express modal meanings. These include *obliger*, *paraître*, *sembler* and *permettre.*

> (65) Car Android de Google et Windows de Microsoft permettent une personnalisation plus poussée, comme sur un PC.
>
> (*Mieux Vivre Votre Argent*, mars 2014)

4.4 Speech acts

Speaking is a form of acting, in the sense that whenever we speak we are doing something, informing, suggesting, praising, sympathizing, and so on. Halliday has suggested that all these acts can be grouped into four types. These four types result from two distinctions. The first relates to the sort of act that is being performed, which can be either one of giving or one of requesting. The second distinction is related to what is given or requested; this can be either information, or goods or services. This gives us the four following possibilities:

1. Giving information

(66) Des millions de personnes dans le monde n'ont jamais recours à la médicine modern allopathique.

(*Marianne*, 25–31 mai 2013)

2. Requesting information

(67) Quand y a-t-il émergence d'une nouvelle sociabilité ?

(Study day programme, 2014)

3. Giving goods or services

(68) Pour ton anniversaire, je t'offre un magazine Bayard Jeunesse à recevoir toute l'année dans ta boîte aux lettres !

(Publicity material, Bayard Jeunesse, 2014)

4. Requesting goods or services

(69) Joindre un chèque du montant de votre cotisation (dans le cas d'une inscription après le congrès de printemps).

(*Bulletin de la SAES*, juin 2004)

This can be expressed diagrammatically as follows:

	Commodity exchanged	
Type of act	*information*	*goods or services*
giving	Des millions de personnes dans le monde n'ont jamais recours à la médicine modern allopathique.	Pour ton anniversaire, je t'offre un magazine Bayard Jeunesse à recevoir toute l'année dans ta boîte aux lettres !
requesting	Quand y a-t-il émergence d'une nouvelle sociabilité ?	Joindre un chèque du montant de votre cotisation (dans le cas d'une inscription après le congrès de printemps).

Summary of chapter 4

- The interpersonal metafunction deals with the relationship established by the speaker.

- The mood structure can be analysed as mood and residue.
  The mood is made up of the finite and the subject.
- An alternative analysis would be in terms of a negotiator and a remainder. The negotiator is made up of the subject, the finite and the predicator.
- Modality can be expressed using a modal auxiliary, which is conjugated, followed by an infinitive.
- The verb *falloir* is used only in the third person, hence it is impersonal.
- Modal adverbs, adjectives, and nouns can also be used to express modality.
- Speech act functions are giving or requesting information or goods or services.

5 Ordering the text

The textual metafunction

In this chapter, we will see how the clause is structured, first in terms of what the speaker takes as his starting point for the message, and, secondly, in terms of what he chooses as his focal point. We will then see how the items that are chosen as starting points throughout a text contribute to the way the text is built up, and thus give it a unified structure. Finally, we will see how these items link together throughout the text, again contributing to its unified structure.

The textual metafunction deals with those aspects of meaning that structure the clause into a meaningful segment of text. The two main types of structure by which this is done are thematic structure and information structure.

5.1 Thematic structure

Thematic structure sees the clause in terms of two components, a theme and a rheme. The theme is defined as the speaker's starting point, and it is realized in French by being placed in initial position in the clause. In the development of the notion of theme, it was sometimes described as being what the clause is about. This definition, however, is vague, and sometimes ambiguous, so that, nowadays, the definition used here, the speaker's starting point, is the one usually given. The rheme is then the development of the theme. Some (e.g. Fawcett 2000) have criticized the notion of rheme on the grounds that it is a negative concept, being, in practice, simply what is not the theme. This claim is not without foundation; but the analysis of the clause in terms of theme and rheme remains valid, and is frequently useful, and, in this book, we will continue to analyse clauses in this way.

The theme has one obligatory component, and this will correspond to the first major grammatical component of the clause; by "major grammatical component" we mean subject, complement, predicator, or circumstantial adjunct. This is known as the topical theme. In certain cases, but not always, the topical theme may be preceded by a linking element, which then functions as textual theme, or by an element indicating the attitude of the speaker, which then functions as an interpersonal theme.

> (70) Dominique de Villepin a créé la surprise en annonçant, dimanche 11 décembre sur TF1, sa candidature à l'élection présidentielle.
>
> (*Le Monde*, 13 décembre 2011)

In this example, it is the grammatical subject, *Dominique de Villepin*, that functions as topical theme.

Dominique de Villepin	a crée la surprise en annonçant, dimanche 11 décembre sur TF1, sa candidature à l'élection présidentielle
Th: Top	Rh

On the other hand, in the following example, it is the circumstantial adjunct *A peine cinq mois après l'investiture d'un nationaliste de gauche à la présidence de Pérou*, that functions as topical theme.

> (71) A peine cinq mois après l'investiture d'un nationaliste de gauche à la présidence de Pérou, cet important remaniement ministériel soulève des interrogations à Lima.
>
> (*Le Monde*, 13 décembre 2011)

A peine cinq mois après l'investiture d'un nationaliste de gauche à la présidence de Pérou	cet important remaniement ministériel soulève des interrogations à Lima
Th: Top	Rh

As a result, the grammatical subject, *cet important remaniement ministeriel*, forms part of the rheme.

A subordinate clause, whether it be finite or non-finite, functions in the same way as a circumstantial adjunct, in the sense that, while having the structure of a clause rather than a group, it has the same semantic function.

> (72) Pour aborder ces questions, un sommet 5+5, réunissant cinq pays du Nord et cinq pays du Sud de la Méditerranée, s'est tenu dimanche 11 décembre à Nouakchott, en Mauritanie.
>
> (*Le Monde*, 13 décembre 2011)

In this example the first component is the non-finite clause, *Pour aborder ces questions*, which thus functions as topical theme.

Pour aborder ces questions	un sommet 5+5, réunissant cinq pays du Nord et cinq pays du Sud de la Méditerranée, s'est tenu dimanche 11 décembre à Nouakchott, en Mauritanie
Th: Top	Rh

In the following example, it is a finite clause that is the initial component.

> (73) Même si la Lorraine est une terre de droite où de nombreux déçus de Nicolas Sarkozy rejoignent le FN, Marine Le Pen a semblé oublier le chef de l'Etat pour uniquement porter ses coups sur la gauche.
>
> (*Le Monde*, 13 décembre 2011)

Hence it is this finite clause that functions as topical theme.

Même si la Lorraine est une terre de droite où de nombreux déçus de Nicolas Sarkozy rejoignent le FN	Marine Le Pen a semblé oublier le chef de l'Etat pour uniquement porter ses coups sur la gauche
Th: Top	Rh

However, this finite clause itself has a clausal structure, and so has its own internal thematic structure, with *Même si* as textual theme, and *la Lorraine* as topical theme. Hence, it is possible to give a more detailed analysis of this clause complex.

Même si	la Lorraine	est une terre de droite où de nombreux déçus de Nicolas Sarkozy rejoignent le FN	Marine Le Pen a semblé oublier le chef de l'Etat pour uniquement porter ses coups sur la gauche
Th: Top			Rh
Th: Txt	Th: Top	Rh	

However, it is important to stress that the second line of this analysis gives only the internal structure of the subordinate clause, which remains, as a whole, the topical theme of the clause complex. Moreover, it might be thought that since the internal structure of the subordinate clause has been analysed in this way, the same thing could be done with the main clause. However, the main clause has an adjunct (the subordinate clause) as part of its structure, and this adjunct is the topical theme. Since only one topical theme per clause is possible, it is not possible to analyse the clause further, which would provide it with a second topical theme.

If a subordinate clause follows the main clause then this functions like an adjunct that occurs within the rheme.

(74) Elles peuvent donc vite sembler dépassées et lasser, si elles ne sont pas associées à des matières et à des teintes plus actuelles.

(*Femme Actuelle*, 9–15 janvier 2012)

This is the case in this example, where the subordinate clause, *si elles ne sont pas associées à des matières et à des teintes plus actuelles*, is within the rheme.

Elles	peuvent donc vite sembler dépassées et lasser, si elles ne sont pas associées à des matières et à des teintes plus actuelles
Th: Top	Rh

However, here again, the subordinate clause does have clausal structure and hence an internal thematic structure that can be analysed.

Elles	peuvent donc vite sembler dépassées et lasser	si	elles	ne sont pas associées à des matières et à des teintes plus actuelles
Th: Top	Rh			
		Th: Txt	Th: Top	Rh

Predicators as theme do not usually occur in declarative clauses, but this would be the normal choice in imperative clauses.

(75) Tapotez dans un champ de saisi texte pour afficher le clavier à l'écran.

(Packard Bell instruction manual, c.2010)

In this example the imperative verb, *Tapotez*, functions as topical theme.

Tapotez	dans un champ de saisi texte pour afficher le clavier à l'écran
Th: Top	Rh

Theoretically, it might be thought that a complement as topical theme should constitute a possibility. However, it would seem that this never occurs in French, since, when a complement is placed in initial position, it is reduplicated by a preposition in its congruent position, thus producing the structure known as left dislocation. Since this fronted complement does not form part of the clause structure, properly so called, it forms an absolute theme. The absolute theme can be considered as a case of preposing the theme, which then functions as theme for the whole of the following clause. The following is an example of this phenomenon.

(76) Ce personnage ambigu, Michel Bouquet l'incarne à la perfection.
(*Femme Actuelle*, 15–21 février 2016)

Here, the complement, *ce personage ambigu*, is separated from the structure of the clause proper, placed in initial position, followed by a comma. Its position in the normal clause structure is replaced by the pronoun *l'*. Thus, there is reduplication of the complement, and *ce personage ambigu*, in initial position, functions as absolute theme. However, the following clause does have clause structure, and so can be said to have an internal thematic structure with *Michel Bouquet* as its topical theme.

Ce personnage ambigu	Michel Bouquet l'incarne à la perfection	
Th: Abs	Rh	
	Th: Top	Rh

In the following example, it is the subject that is preposed as absolute theme.

(77) Le troisième élément de l'accord, c'est un effort de discipline, avec une majorité inversée pour les sanctions automatiques.
(*Le Monde*, 13 décembre 2011)

Le troisième élément de l'accord	c'est un effort de discipline, avec une majorité inversée pour les sanctions automatiques
Th: Abs	Rh

However, to the extent that the clause, *c'est un effort de discipline, avec une majorité inversée pour les sanctions automatiques*, does have a genuine clause structure, it could be said, as in the previous example, to have an internal thematic structure of its own, where *c'* is the topical theme of this structure.

Le troisième élément de l'accord	c'	est un effort de discipline, avec une majorité inversée pour les sanctions automatiques
Th: Abs	Rh	
	Th: Top	Rh

However, it must be emphasized that c' is the theme only of the internal structure of this clause and that it remains part of the rheme of the clause as a whole.

In written French, this occurs in the "c'est" type like the above example, and in polar questions with a nominal, as opposed to a pronominal, subject, but otherwise is rare. On the other hand, over the last 20 years or so, it has become exceedingly common in spoken French.

There are two other types of theme that can contribute to the thematic material, but that are not obligatory, in the sense that they sometimes occur, but sometimes do not. These are interpersonal theme and textual theme. If interpersonal themes occur, they precede the topical theme. The topical theme always terminates the thematic material of the clause; hence if a lexical item, which could have functioned as interpersonal theme, occurs after the topical theme, it is part of the rheme, not part of the theme. Interpersonal themes relate to the relationship either between the speaker and his addressees, or between the speaker and his message.

(78) Sommes-nous condamnés à voir notre système social se degrader ?
(*Le Monde*, 13 décembre 2011)

In this example the auxiliary verb *sommes*, signals that the clause is interrogative, and so attributes the role of questioner to the speaker, and the role of potential answerer to the addressee; hence its function is related to the relationship between speaker and hearer. As such it is an interpersonal theme. But as an interpersonal theme, it does not exhaust the thematic material, and so, the following component, *nous*, which functions as grammatical subject, is the topical theme.

Sommes-	nous	condamnés à voir notre système social se degrader ?
Th: Inter	The: Top	Rh

In the following example, *Certes* indicates that the speaker is making a concession, and hence indicates his attitude towards the content of the clause.

(79) Certes, la forme juridique que prendra cet accord reste floue.
(*Le Monde*, 13 décembre 2011)

Certes, therefore, is an interpersonal theme, and the following component, the grammatical subject, *la form juridique que prendra cet accord*, is the topical theme.

Certes	la forme juridique que prendra cet accord	reste floue
Th: Inter	Th: Top	Rh

In a similar way, *Heureusement* gives the judgement of the speaker on the content of the following clause, and so indicates his attitude; it is thus an interpersonal theme, and the following grammatical subject, *certains*, is the topical theme.

(80) Heureusement, certains gardent les pieds sur terre.
(*Le Monde*, 13 décembre 2011)

Heureusement	certains	gardent les pieds sur terre
Th: Inter	Th: Top	Rh

The second type of optional theme is textual theme. These are initial elements, preceding the topical theme, whose function is to link the clause to the rest of the discourse. In the following sequence, the thematic structure of the third clause complex begins with the conjunction *Et*, which functions as a textual theme; this is followed by the adjunct, *en cette matière comme en d'autres*, which constitutes the topical theme.

(81) Heureusement, certains gardent les pieds sur terre. Notamment ces "survivalistes", qui se préparent chaque jour au pire. Et en cette matière comme en d'autres, les Américains cultivent un certain professionnalisme là où les français demeurent des amateurs.
(*Le Monde*, 13 décembre 2011)

The thematic structure of the third clause complex is thus:

Et	en cette matière comme en d'autres	les Américains cultivent un certain professionnalisme là où les français demeurent des amateurs
Th: Txt	Th: Top	Rh

We saw above, in the discussion on adjuncts as theme, that a subordinate clause that precedes the main clause can function as topical theme, just like an initial circumstantial adjunct. However, when two clauses are in conjunction, they constitute separate clause complexes and each has its own thematic structure.

(82) Nous les enveloppons dans de couvertures de survie et un premier bilan est effectué à l'attention du CROSS.

(SNSM leaflet, c.2008)

Here the two clauses can be analysed separately:

Nous	les enveloppons dans de couvertures de survie
Th: Top	Rh

et	un premier bilan	est effectué à l'attention du CROSS
Th: Txt	Th: top	Rh

However, in cases like this, where the subject of the two clauses is identical, it is frequent for the subject of the second clause not to be expressed. How are such cases to be treated? There seem to be three possibilities: first, one can reinstate the "elided" subject, and then analyse them as two separate clauses, as above; secondly, it is possible to treat the second clause as written, but without altering it, in which case it will be the first main component expressed, usually the verb, which will be analysed as topical theme; thirdly, one can treat the subject of the first clause as being the theme for the total segment that follows even though this segment, structurally, comprises two clauses. Thus, in the segment below, there are two coordinate clauses, but the subject of the first, *Un voilier*, is understood as being also the subject of the second.

(83) Un voilier nous approche et nous signale deux enfants faisant de grands signes sur une embarcation à environ 1,5 mille de notre position.

(SNSM leaflet, c.2008)

The first option would involve altering the clause as it appears. The second option would give *Un voilier* as topical theme of the first clause, but *nous* as topical theme of the second. This seems curious, and inconsistent. The third option, which we prefer, gives the following analysis.

Un voilier	nous approche et nous signale deux enfants faisant de grands signes sur une embarcation à environ 1,5 mille de notre position
Th: Top	Rh

This is simple, but more importantly, it seems to me, intuitively correct.

There are a small number of constructions that need to be treated differently. This applies mainly to cleft and extraposed structures.

(84) C'est pour lutter contre cet état d'esprit, individualiste et égoïste que nous avons mis en place la Charte du Citoyen de la Mer.

(SNSM leaflet, c.2008)

This is an example of a cleft structure, where the adjunct, *pour lutter contre cet état d'esprit, individualiste et égoïste*, has been clefted and placed in initial position. This is a strategy for placing a component in theme position, and thus the cleft segment is considered to be the topical theme.

C'est pour lutter contre cet état d'esprit, individualiste et égoïste	que nous avons mis en place la Charte du Citoyen de le Mer
Th: Top	Rh

The following is an example of extraposition.

(85) Il est important de souligner que l'hygiène intime n'est pas nécessairement réservé qu'aux filles.

(*Bien Etre & Santé*, février 2007)

The subject of this clause is expressed twice, once as the pronoun *Il*, and once as the extraposed clause, *de souligner que l'hygiène intime n'est pas nécessairement réservé qu'aux filles*. Here, it is the extraposition matrix, *Il est important*, that is placed in initial position, and thus functions as theme.

Il est important	de souligner que l'hygiène intime n'est pas nécessairement réservé qu'aux filles
Th: Top	Rh

Relative clauses provide a peculiar situation, since the relative pronoun links the relative clause to the main clause, and so functions as a textual theme; at the same time, it functions as a component with the relative clause, usually as subject or complement, and so functions as topical theme. The relative pronoun thus has the peculiarity of having a dual function. However, since the relative clause is always rankshifted within the group of which its antecedent is the head, this only occurs within the internal structure of the relative clause itself.

(86) Photographiée par Judy Linn, la rockeuse livre ses secrets à travers cette série de portraits qui couvrent près d'une décennie.

(*Femme actuelle*, 9–15 janvier 2012)

<table>
<tr><td>Photographiée par Judy Linn, la rockeuse</td><td>livre ses secrets à travers cette série de portraits</td><td>qui</td><td>couvrent près d'une décennie</td></tr>
<tr><td>Th: Top</td><td colspan="3">Rh</td></tr>
<tr><td></td><td></td><td>Th: Txt/Top</td><td>Rh</td></tr>
</table>

5.2 Analysis of an authentic example

The following text occurs in a short book on the town of Rennes intended for tourists (Pierre Dechifre & Gilbert Lebrun: *Rennes*, Editions Ouest-France, 2002).

> Anne de Bretagne n'a que 11 ans lorsqu'elle hérite du duché de Bretagne, lequel suscite de multiples convoitises. Le roi Charles VIII s'est emparé de Nantes et de Guingamp, ses troupes assiègent Rennes. Pour sauver ce qui peut l'être, la petite duchesse, instruite et volontaire, consent à épouser le roi de France. Ce qui sera fait le 6 décembre 1491.
>
> Le contrat de mariage prévoit qu'en toute hypothèse, la Bretagne restera possession du royaume. La mort de Charles VIII, en avril 1498, la replace provisoirement à la tête du duché jusqu'à son nouveau mariage avec Louis XII. Des huit enfants nés de ces deux mariages, seules deux filles lui survivront : Renée et Claude, future épouse de François 1er.

<table>
<tr><td>Anne de Bretagne</td><td>n'a que 11 ans</td><td>lorsqu'</td><td>elle</td><td>hérite du duché de Bretagne</td><td>lequel</td><td>suscite de multiples convoitises</td></tr>
<tr><td>Th: Top</td><td colspan="6">Rh</td></tr>
<tr><td></td><td></td><td>Th: Txt</td><td>Th: Top</td><td colspan="3">Rh</td></tr>
<tr><td></td><td></td><td></td><td></td><td></td><td>Th: Txt/Top</td><td>Rh</td></tr>
</table>

The first clause complex of this text has *Anne de Bretagne* as its topical theme. The rheme has a subordinate clause within it, whose topical theme is *elle*, preceded by the textual theme *lorsqu'*. This in turn has a rankshifted relative clause, with *lequel* functioning as both textual and topical theme. The following clauses are simpler.

Le roi Charles VIII	s'est emparé de Nantes et de Guingamp
Th: Top	Rh

ses troupes	assiègent Rennes
Th: Top	Rh

Despite the fact that the printed text has only a comma between these two segments, they function as separate clauses.

Pour sauver ce	qui	peut l'être	la petite duchesse, instruite et volontaire consent à épouser le roi de France
Th: Top			Rh
	Th: Txt/Top	Rh	

The topical theme of this clause is the adjunct, *Pour sauver ce qui peut l'être*, but this has a relative clause rankshifted within it, whose internal structure has a combined textual and topical theme, *qui*.

Ce qui	sera fait le 6 décembre 1491
Th: Top	Rh

Had this been preceded by a comma rather than a full stop, it would have been natural to treat it as a relative clause within the previous clause complex. However, the punctuation has given it clausal status, and that is how it has been analysed here.

Le contrat de mariage	prévoit	qu'	en toute hypothèses	la Bretagne restera possession du royaume
Th: Top	Rh			
		Th: Txt	Th: Top	Rh

This clause contains a rankshifted clause, whose internal structure has *qu'* as textual theme and the adjunct, *en toute hypothèse*, as topical theme. The two final clauses, though perhaps longer than those preceding them, are relatively simple from the point of view of their thematic structure.

La mort de Charles VIII en avril 1498,	la replace provisoirement à la tête du duché jusqu'à son nouveau mariage avec Louis XII
Th: Top	Rh

Des huit enfants nés de ces deux mariages	seules deux filles lui survivront : Renée et Claude, future épouse de François 1er
Th: Top	Rh

5.3 Thematic progression

The importance of theme is not simply a question of its significance within the clause. It also has an important role in the relationships between clauses. The ways in which a theme is derived from the preceding discourse constitutes a significant element in the construction of the argumentation of the text, and this is called thematic progression. There are basically two ways in which this derivation can take place; the first is where the theme is derived from a previous theme in the discourse. This is called constant progression. Alternatively, a theme can be derived from a previous rheme in the discourse. This is called linear progression. Many commentators claim that there is a third type of theme, usually called hypertheme, where a theme cannot be related to a specific theme or rheme in the previous discourse, but is related to a more general idea that the text is about. While this is to a certain extent true, the hypertheme does not seem to be of the same order as constant and linear progression. Themes in constant and linear progression may well also be related to a hypertheme, so it does not constitute a third possibility; it is at a different level. Of course, it is always possible to have a theme that is unrelated to the previous discourse, since a speaker is always free to introduce a new element into his discourse and use it as the starting point of a new clause. This frequently, but not necessarily, happens at the beginning of a new paragraph.

In natural language, it is fairly rare to find an extended passage which has only constant, or only linear progression; however, texts of simple description or narration will tend to have more examples of constant than linear progression, while texts of a more argumentative nature will tend to have more linear than constant progression.

The following text is a biographical note following an academic article in the journal *ASp, la revue du GERAS*, No.60, 2011.

Marion Bendinelli est doctorante à l'Université de Nice Sophia-Antipolis où elle est Attachée Temporaire d'Enseignement et de

Recherche en linguistique générale. Elle appartient à l'UMR 6039, "Bases, Corpus, Langage". Ses travaux portent sur l'expression de la modalité en anglais dans le cadre de la communication persuasive, et en particulier, au sein des débats présidentiels américains. Ses questions de recherche se situent dans le champ de l'analyse de discours politique, de la logométrie, de la linguistique énonciative et de la linguistique interactionnelle.

The following is an analysis of the thematic structure including the thematic progression. Note that the thematic progression only concerns the topical themes of the ranking clauses, that is, the clauses at the first level of the thematic structure analysis.

Th1 ⇨ Rh1	Marion Bendinelli	est doctorante à l'Université de Nice Sophia-Antipolis	où	elle est Attachée Temporaire d'Enseignement et de Recherche en linguistique générale
	Th: Top	Rh		
			Th: Txt/Top	Rh

In the first clause, the proper name, *Marion Bendinelli* functions as subject and as topical theme. The rest of the clause functions as rheme; but this rheme includes the adverbial relative clause introduced by *où*; in the internal structure of this relative clause, *où* functions as both textual and topical theme, with the rest of the relative clause as rheme.

⇩ Th2 ⇨ Rh2	Elle	appartient à l'UMR 6039, "Bases, Corpus, Langage"
	Th: Top	Rh

In the following clause, *Elle* functions as topical theme. This pronoun is co-referential with the theme of the previous clause and so is derived from it. Thus, we have an instance of constant theme symbolized by the vertical arrow.

⇩ Th3 ⇨ Rh3	Ses travaux	portent sur l'expression de la modalité en anglais dans le cadre de la communication persuasive, et en particulier, au sein des débats présidentiels américains
	Th: Top	Rh

The topical theme of the third clause is *Ses travaux*. While this is not a simple repetition of the previous theme, the work in question is that of the person who is theme of the previous clause; So, this theme can be said to be derived from the theme of the previous clause, and so is again an example of constant theme.

⇩ Th4 ⇨ Rh4	Ses questions de recherche	se situent dans le champ de l'analyse de discours politique, de la logométrie, de la linguistique énonciative et de la linguistique interactionnelle
	Th: Top	Rh

The topical theme of the final clause, *Ses questions de recherche*, derives from *Ses travaux*, theme of the previous clause, providing yet another constant link.

Hence this short text provides an example of a simple descriptive text where all the thematic links are of the constant type.

The following is a little more complex and is taken from a tourist booklet of 2004 for Finistère:

> La pêche en eau douce séduit les amoureux de la nature tout comme les amateurs de pêche sportive. Chaque parcours de pêche invite à sa façon à la découverte du patrimoine finistérien : flore faune, paysage. . . Grâce à une gestion rigoureuse de l'environnement, rivières, lacs et cours d'eau sont entretenus et protégés. Dans ces eaux claires et vives, les espèces se reproduisent naturellement et peuplent les rivières de poissons sauvages. Plus de 4 500 km de cours d'eau sont classés en première catégorie piscicole.
>
> La diversité des lieux de pêche est propice à la prolifération d'une grande variété d'espèces dont les plus recherchées sont la truite fario, le brochet et le saumon atlantique, Eog en breton.

An analysis of the thematic structure and progression follows.

Th1 ⇨ Rh1	La pêche en eau douce	séduit les amoureux de la nature tout comme les amateurs de pêche sportive
	Th: Top	Rh

⇩ Th2 ⇨ Rh2	Chaque parcours de pêche	invite à sa façon à la découverte du patrimoine finistérien : flore faune, paysage. . .
	Th: Top	Rh

The first clause is made up of the first theme (Th1) followed by the first rheme (Rh1). In the second clause, the topical theme *Chaque parcours de pêche*, is derived from *La pêche en eau douce*, the topical theme of the first clause. This is an example of constant progression, symbolized by the vertical arrow above Th2.

<table>
<tr><td rowspan="2">⇙
Th3 ⇨ Rh3</td><td>Grâce à une gestion rigoureuse de l'environnement</td><td>rivières, lacs et cours d'eau sont entretenus et protégés</td></tr>
<tr><td>Th: Top</td><td>Rh</td></tr>
</table>

In the third clause, the adjunct, *Grâce à une gestion rigureuse de l'environnement*, follows on from the mention of *flore, faune, paysage* in the preceding rheme; this is then an example of linear progression symbolized by the oblique arrow above Th3.

<table>
<tr><td rowspan="2">⇙
Th4 ⇨ Rh4</td><td>Dans ces eaux claires et vives</td><td>les espèces se reproduisent naturellement et peuplent les rivières de poissons sauvages</td></tr>
<tr><td>Th: Top</td><td>Rh</td></tr>
</table>

The fourth clause also has an adjunct as its topical theme. Although *Dans ces eaux claires et vives*, has a relationship with the themes 1 and 2, this passes through the rheme of clause three in the form of *rivières, lacs et cours d'eau*. Hence the progression is again linear.

<table>
<tr><td rowspan="2">⇩
Th5 ⇨ Rh5</td><td>Plus de 4 500 km de cours d'eau</td><td>sont classés en première catégorie piscicole</td></tr>
<tr><td>Th: Top</td><td>Rh</td></tr>
</table>

The subject functions as topical theme in the fifth clause, and this derives from the preceding theme thus forming a constant link.

<table>
<tr><td rowspan="2">⇩
Th6 ⇨ Rh6</td><td>La diversité des lieux de pêche</td><td>est propice à la prolifération d'une grande variété d'espèces</td><td>dont les plus recherchées</td><td>sont la truite fario, le brochet et le saumon atlantique, Eog en breton</td></tr>
<tr><td>Th: Top</td><td colspan="3">Rh</td></tr>
<tr><td></td><td></td><td></td><td>Th: Txt/Top</td><td>Rh</td></tr>
</table>

Despite the fact that there is a paragraph break, the final clause of our extract has a topical theme derived from the previous topical theme, which therefore constitutes another constant link. The rheme incorporates a relative clause whose subject, *dont les plus recherchées*, is both a textual and a topical theme of the relative clause's internal structure. However, the relative clause is not a ranking clause, and so this does not enter into the thematic progression.

Here there are three constant links and two linear links, so the extract as a whole leans towards the constant type. It will be noted that items linked to themes appear in rhemes; this would be dealt with in a more general analysis of cohesion, to which thematic progression can be thought as being a part. Nevertheless, such links do not play a part in thematic progression as such.

The following extract is rather more complex. It is the beginning of the Introduction from *Les auxiliaries être et avoir* by Pierre-Don Giancarli, published by the Presses Universitaires de Rennes in 2011.

Nous nous appuierons sur un corpus authentique comptant au total plus de 2 millions de mots (2 082 084), comprenant un corpus d'acadien traditionnel, un corpus trilingue français-corse-anglais, et divers corpus bilingues (française-corse, corse-française, français-anglais, anglais-français).

Le corpus d'acadien est le corpus Péronnet dit "85" : il s'agit d'un corpus d'acadien traditionnel (75000 mots) réalisé dans le sud-est de la province du Nouveau-Brunswick (seul province du Canada officiellement bilingue anglais-français) à partir de sept informateurs âgés et ruraux, qui sont nés et habitent dans des villages à forte majorité francophone, dorénavant nommés de INF1 à INF7, et qui racontent des contes et légendes. Leurs anglicismes sont intégrés et anciens, moins dus à des contacts individuels avec l'anglais qu'à une influence exercée dès le début : l'Acadie, revendiquée par la France en 1534 avec des implantions françaises dès 1604, fut la première colonie française en Amérique.

Le corpus trilingue, que nous avons constitué et aligné et qui n'est sans doute pas loin d'être exhaustif dans ce domaine, comporte 195 478 mots en anglais, correspondant à 222 733 mots en corse et à 280 972 mots en français.

The following is a possible analysis.

Th1 ⇨ Rh1	Nous	nous appuierons sur un corpus authentique comptant au total plus de 2 millions de mots (2 082 084), comprenant un corpus d'acadien traditionnel, un corpus trilingue français-corse-anglais, et divers corpus bilingues (française-corse, corse-française, français-anglais, anglais-français).
	Th: Top	Rh

The first clause is relatively simple, despite the long rheme, with the grammatical subject, *Nous*, functioning as topical theme.

⬀ Th2 ⇨ Rh2	Le corpus d'acadien	est le corpus Péronnet dit "85"
	Th: Top	Rh

The theme of the second clause, Le corpus d'acadien, is derived from Rh1, giving a linear link.

⬀ Th3 ⇨ Rh3	il	s'agit d'un corpus d'acadien traditionnel (75000 mots) réalisé dans le sud-est de la province du Nouveau-Brunswick (seul province du Canada officiellement bilingue anglais-français) à partir de sept informateurs âgés et ruraux,	qui	sont nés et abitant dans des villages à forte majorité francophone, dorénavant nommés de INF1 à INF7	et	qui	racontent des contes et légendes
	Th: Top	Rh					
			Th: Txt/ Top	Rh	Th: Txt	Th: Txt/ Top	Rh

The pronoun, *il*, which functions as theme, refers back to *le corpus Péronnet* in the previous rheme, thus the link is linear. The rheme also incorporates two relative clauses that are themselves coordinate. These are thus at the same level, each having a relative pronoun functioning as both textual and topical theme; the second relative clause in addition has a separate textual theme in *et*. Note that *et* provides a textual link to the previous relative clause, while *qui* links the relative clause to its antecedent.

⇗ Th4 ⇨ Rh4	Leurs anglicismes	sont intégrés et anciens, moins dus à des contacts individuels avec l'anglais qu'à une influence exercée dès le début
	Th: Top	Rh

The theme of the fourth clause, *Leurs anglicismes*, is linked to the previous rheme, since the *anglicismes* in question are those of the *sept informateurs* of Rh3. So once again we have a linear link.

⇗ (from Rh3) Th5 ⇨ Rh5	l'Acadie, revendiquée par la France en 1534 avec des implantions françaises dès 1604	fut la première colonie française en Amérique
	Th: Top	Rh

The theme of this clause is *l'Acadie . . .* In a sense this notion is present throughout the extract, but, in terms of the text, it last appeared through the language, *acadien*, mentioned in Rh3. We can thus say that textually the derivation is through a linear link not from the immediately preceding rheme, but from Rh3.

⇗ (from Rh1) Th6 ⇨ Rh6	Le corpus trilingue	que	nous avons constitué et aligné	et	qui	n'est sans doute pas loin d'être exhaustif dans ce domaine	comporte 195 478 mots en anglais, correspondant à 222 733 mots en corse et à 280 972 mots en français
	Th: top						Rh
		Th: Top	Rh	Th: Txt	Th: Top	Rh	

The first clause of the next paragraph takes us back to the first clause of the extract, but taken up again as the theme *Le corpus trilingue* mentioned in the first rheme. The theme also has two coordinate relative clauses, like the rheme of the third clause.

Hence it can be seen that the thematic progression of this extract is linear. Even though not all the links are directly from the immediately preceding rheme, they are from preceding rhemes, though these may be further away in the text. This shows how the argument structure of this text is being built up.

5.4 Information structure

Just as thematic structure is involved with the way the text is constructed, information structure is concerned with the structure of a text. Hence, they have a certain similarity, and have sometimes been confused. However, they do have a very important difference: they do not apply to the same unit. We have seen that the unit of thematic structure is the clause; the unit of information structure is not the clause, but the tone unit. The tone unit is a phonological unit whose main characteristic is to have one tonic stress. In simple cases, the clause and the tone unit may coincide, which is why they have sometimes been confused, but in natural language, they frequently differ. Consider the following example:

(87) On nous a volé notre cadeau de Noël.

(*Le Monde*, 13 décembre 2011)

It would be possible to conceive of this clause being uttered with a single tonic accent on the final word *Noël*. In this case, there would be a single tone unit, and the clause and tone unit would coincide. However, it would be equally possible to imagine this clause being uttered with two tonic accents, one on *volé*, and the other on *Noël*. In this case, there would be two tone units: *On nous a volé*, and *notre cadeau de Noël*. But there is still only one clause. So, although there is one clause, there are, in this case, two tone units. Consequently, the tone unit and clause are not the same, and do not necessarily coincide.

Within the tone unit, information structure distinguishes between the given and the focalized (often referred to as the new). The focalized is identified as being the element where the tonic accent is placed. If, for the sake of argument, we take the above example, with a single tonic accent on *Noël*, this element would be focalized, the beginning of the tone unit would be given, but, out of context, it would not be possible to tell precisely where the given ends and the focalized begins. This could be symbolized as follows:

On nous a volé notre cadeau de Noël.
Given ← Focalized

The arrow indicates that the focalized stretches back to some unspecified point in the tone unit. For example, if the situation was that only the fact that something had been stolen from us was known, then the focalized would include *notre cadeau de Noël*. If it was simply known that something had happened to us, then the focalized would include *a volé notre cadeau de Noël*. The case of the tonic accent falling on the final element is the most common case.

If the tonic accent falls on an item other than the final item, then the effect is one of contrast. If in this case the single tonic accent were to fall on *volé*, this would mean that what had happened to our Christmas present was that it was stolen rather than something different – lost, for example. If the single tonic accent fell on *nous*, this would mean that the Christmas present that was stolen was ours rather than someone else's.

5.5 Analysis of an authentic example

Since information structure depends on the placement of the tonic accent, it applies primarily to spoken language, but that does not mean it is absent in written language. When we read, we mentally attribute tonic accents, and hence an information structure, to the text. However, this means that the information structure of a piece of written language depends on the person reading it, and there may be variations from reader to reader. The following is an extract from a written text (even though it is intended to simulate a spoken text) that appeared in *Femme Actuelle*, 3–9 février 2014.

> Cette pièce couronne une longue et belle histoire d'amitié ?
> Laurent Ruquier et moi, on se connait depuis l'émission *Rien à Cirer* sur France Inter. En quinze ans d'amitié, Laurent s'est rarement livré à moi. On peut même dire que notre complicité est née sous le manteau !

In this analysis, the words that would carry the tonic accent in my reading are in bold.

Cette pièce	couronne une longue et belle histoire **d'amitié** ?
Given	← Focalized

Laurent Ruquier	et **moi**
Given	← Focalized

on	se connait depuis l'émission *Rien à* ***Cirer***
Given	← Focalized

	sur France **Inter**
Given	← Focalized

This piece of supplementary information has no given element.

	En quinze ans **d'amitié**
Given	← Focalized

This introductory piece of information has no given element.

Laurent	s'est rarement livré à **moi**.
Given	← Focalized

On	peut même **dire**
Given	← Focalized

que notre complicité	est née sous le **manteau** !
Given	← Focalized

The segments here are tone units, which may, but do not necessarily, correspond to clauses. So, although thematic structure and information structure are related, they do not necessarily map onto one another. The following shows how these would be related in this extract.

Cette pièce	couronne une longue et belle histoire **d'amitié** ?
Th. Top	Rh.
Given	← Focalized

Laurent Ruquier	et **moi**	on	se connait depuis l'émission *Rien à* ***Cirer***	sur France **Inter**
Th. Abs		Rh.		
Given	← Focalized	Given	← Focalized	← Focalized

In the first clause, the thematic structure and the information structure do map onto one another, with the subject, *Cette pièce*, functioning as both theme and given. The second clause is divided into three tone units, so the two types of structure do not map onto one another in this case. The theme, *Laurent Ruquier et moi*, constitutes a tone unit in itself and so has a given and a focalized; the rheme is itself divided into two tone units, the first with a given and focalized, the second with only a focalized element.

En quinze ans **d'amitié**	Laurent	s'est rarement livré à **moi**
Th. Top	Rh.	
← Focalized	Given	← Focalized

This clause is divided into two tone units. The first has only a focalized, and the second, corresponding to the rheme, has a given and a focalized.

On	peut même **dire**	que notre complicité	est née sous le **manteau** !
Th. Top	Rh.		
Given	← Focalized	Given	← Focalized

In this final clause of the extract, the clause is again divided into two tone units, but here, the theme corresponds to the given of the first tone unit, and the rheme includes the focalized of the first and the given and focalized of the second.

5.6 Cohesion

Cohesion is the linguistic phenomenon that links different items in the text together, so that the clauses are not simply a sequence of clauses, but are knit into a unit that we call a text. One of the most important types of cohesion is reference, by which it is possible to refer to an item earlier or later in the text, or an item in the outside world that addressees can be expected to recognize. References to items within the text are said to be endophoric; these can be divided into those that refer to items earlier in the text, which are said to be anaphoric, and those that refer to items later in the text, said to be cataphoric. Consider the following example.

> (88) Simone a 80 ans, et à la table à coté, trois clients plutôt éméchés parlent de préparer un cambriolage ! Ils lui demandent si elle voudra bien faire le guet.
>
> (*Fémina*, 22–28 septembre 2014)

There are three examples of anaphora in the second sentence of this example. The pronoun *ils* refers back to *trois clients*; and both *lui* and *elle* refer back to *Simone*. It is easy to imagine how cumbersome this segment would be if the resource of reference did not exist!

In the following example the possessive pronoun *ses* refers to *notre fille* in the following clause. This is an example of cataphora.

> (89) Ayant suivi ses études en Australie, notre fille a rencontré quelqu'un de très sympathique.
>
> (*Fémina*, 22–28 septembre 2014)

References to items in the real world, outside the text, are called exophora. In the following example, *la Bourse* can be said to be an example of exophora.

> (90) Cette manifestation qui se tient tous les ans à la Bourse est la seule au monde consacré exclusivement au dessin.
>
> (*Mieux Vivre Votre Argent*, mars 2014)

The reference is to the French Stock Exchange. Although there are many stock exchanges in the world, in this context, a French magazine dealing with economic matters, *la Bourse*, without any other qualification, can only possibly refer to the French Stock Exchange, and this would be understood by all readers of the magazine.

5.7 Analysis of an authentic example

Consider the following text (*Femme Actuelle*, 3–9 février 2014):

> Pour les stages de plus de six mois, les jeunes peuvent désormais valider deux trimestres avec une cotisation réduite et échelonnée. Par exemple, ils ont le droit de valider un trimestre en déboursant 12,50 € par mois pendant deux ans. Progrès aussi pour les jeunes qui multiplient les petits boulots : ceux-ci vont plus facilement compter pour la retraite, car la rémunération minimale pour valider un trimestre est ramenée de 200 fois le smic horaire à 150 fois (1 429,50 €).

Using the following symbols:

Anaphora: ↖
Cataphora: ↗
Exophora: ↑

the text can be analysed as follows:

↗ ↑

Pour les stages de plus de six mois, les jeunes peuvent désormais valider deux trimestres

↖ ↗

avec une cotisation réduite et échelonnée. Par exemple, ils ont le droit de valider un

↗

trimestre en déboursant 12,50 € par mois pendant deux ans. Progrès aussi pour les

↑ ↖ ↑

jeunes qui multiplient les petits boulots : ceux-ci vont plus facilement compter pour la

↗

retraite, car la rémunération minimale pour valider un trimestre est ramenée de 200 fois

↑

le smic horaire à 150 fois (1 429,50 €).

The definite article tells us that the addressee is expected to be able to identify what is being talked about. In the case of *les stages*, this is explained in the qualifier *de plus de six mois*, and so is considered a case of cataphora because its reference is made explicit by a following phrase. In the case of *les jeunes*, it is evident that the young people in question are those in France who are in work placements; so this is an example of exophora. The pronoun *ils* refers back to *les jeunes*; this is an example of anaphora. *Le droit* is made explicit in the following phrase (cataphora). The same can be said of the second occurrence of *les jeunes*. It can be noted that this occurrence of *les jeunes* refers to a more restricted group than the first occurrence. *Les petits boulots* is cataphoric, referring to a phenomenon of contemporary society. *Ceux-ci* is anaphoric referring back to (the second occurrence of) *les jeunes*. *La retraite* is obviously exophoric. *La remuneration minimale* is an example of cataphora, again made explicit in the following qualifying phrase. *Le smic* is the French minimum wage, and hence known to all readers of the magazine: a case of exophora.

5.8 Lexical chains

Cohesion is also created by the use of lexical chains. Throughout a text, chains can be built up by the repetition of words, by using words that have the same or similar meanings, or simply words that cluster round a single notion. In the following sequence, the repetition of the word *fondation* contributes to the cohesion of the passage.

> (91) La **fondation** a indiqué qu'elle n'accepterait à l'avenir que des contributions de six Etats (Allemagne, Autriche, Canada, Norvège,

Pays-Bas et Royaume-Uni) dont les relations avec les Etats-Unis sont au dessous de tout soupçon.

Alors que la candidate Clinton (qui a démissionné du conseil d'administration de la **fondation**) se préoccupe de la situation de la classe moyenne, grande oubliée de la reprise économique, les enquêtes décrivent un univers assez éloigné du débat sur le niveau du salaire minimum . . .

(*Le Monde*, 8 mai 2015)

However, it should be noted that French style tends to avoid repetition, so this resource is used less in French than in some other languages. The following might be taken to be a case in point, where *Nicolas Sarkozy* and *l'ancien chef d'état* refer to the same person.

(92) Dans sa bataille contre les juges, **Nicolas Sarkozy** a perdu, jeudi 7 mai, une manche très importante devant la cour d'appel de Paris. La chambre de l'instruction a en effet validé l'essentiel des écoutes téléphoniques à l'origine de la mise en examen de **l'ancien chef d'état**, le 2 juillet 2014, pour "corruption active", "trafic d'influence actif" et "recel de violation de secret professionnel".

(*Le Monde*, 8 mai 2015)

In the following extract the words *mandat* and *candidature* could be thought of as belonging to the same lexical set, that of democratically elected functions. In a democratic system, candidates put themselves up for election and, if elected, they have a mandate.

(93) Le président Pierre Nkurunziza a réaffirmé mercredi 6 mai, qu'il briguera un troisième **mandat** le 26 juin. Des manifestations contre cette **candidature** se déroulent depuis plus de dix jours dans la capitale, Bujumbura.

(*Le Monde*, 8 mai 2015)

5.9 Analysis of an authentic example

In a longer text these lexical chains can be used to draw out the verbal semantic strings that show how the text hangs together, and creates its own texture. Consider the following report from the international news section of a local newspaper (*Le Télégramme*, 3 mars 2015).

> Des policiers de Los Angeles ont tué, dimanche, un homme – probablement un sans-abri –, a annoncé, hier, la police de la ville, après la diffusion d'images de la scène sur internet. La vidéo, publiée sur Facebook, montre une violente altercation entre un homme et plusieurs policiers dans le quartier défavorisé de Skid Row, proche du centre ville. La police a expliqué que l'homme avait été pris pour cible par trois policiers, après avoir tenté de saisir de l'arme de l'un d'entre eux. Deux policiers ont été légèrement blessés, et ceux qui ont tiré sur l'homme ont été écartés du terrain pour le moment, a précisé le porte-parole de la police de Los Angeles, le commandant Andrew Smith.

This text has several semantic strings, the most important of which is that relating to the police, and that contains ten elements: *Des policiers – la police – plusieurs policiers – La police – trois policiers – l'un d'entre eux – Deux policiers – ceux qui – la police – le commandant*. The other main strings associated with this are those of violence: *ont tué – une violente altercation – cible – l'arme – ont été blessés – ont tire*; and the anonymous victim: *un homme – un homme – l'homme – l'homme*. One string also situates the action described in the text: *Los Angeles – la ville – proche du centre ville – Los Angeles*. A shorter string, with only three elements, is nevertheless significant because of the elements being strategically placed at the beginning, middle and end of the text; this string relates to the police's attempt to explain the shooting: *a annoncé – a expliqué – a precisé*. It is also possible to find shorter strings, which may be limited to just one part of the text, such as that of images: *images – video*, or the Internet: *internet – Facebook*, which, although shorter still, help to bind the text together. These strings are set out in the columns of the following table, where the various elements are set out from left to right as they occur in the text.

The police	*The town*	*violence*	*A man*	*Explanation*	*Images*	*Internet*
policiers	Los Angeles	ont tué	un homme	a annoncé		
↓	↓	↓	↓	↓		
la police	la ville				images	internet
↓	↓				↓	↓
					video	Facebook
		altercation	un homme			
policiers	centre-ville		↓			
↓	↓					
la police				a expliqué		
↓				↓		
			l'homme			
			↓			
		cible				
		↓				
3 policiers		l'arme				
↓		↓				
l'un						
↓						
2 policiers		été blessés				
↓		↓				
ceux		ont tiré	l'homme	a précisé		
↓						
la police	Los Angeles					
↓						
commandant						

This is not necessarily exhaustive. Some readers might find other strings in the text, but the main ones have been given here, and this is sufficient to show that these semantic strings create a web of meaning that stretches across the text and helps make it into a meaningful unit.

Summary of chapter 5

- The textual metafunction deals with the ways in which the clause is structured.
- Thematic structure distinguishes between a theme and a rheme.
- The theme is the starting point of the clause, and is placed at the beginning.
- The clause always has a topical theme, which is the first main constituent (subject, adjunct, complement or predicator).
- It may optionally also have textual and/or interpersonal themes.
- Absolute theme is a theme that is separated from the clause structure proper.
- Thematic progression is the way in which the themes are related throughout a text.
- Constant progression occurs when a theme is derived from a previous theme.

- Linear progression occurs when a theme is derived from a previous rheme.
- Information structure has the tone unit (not the clause) as its unit.
- It distinguishes between the given and the focalized.
- The focalized is identified by the position of the tonic accent.
- Cohesion deals with the ways in which a text is linked together.
- Endophoric links are links within the text, and can be anaphoric or cataphoric.
- Anaphoric links are links to something previously mentioned in the text.
- Cataphoric links are links to something which follows in the text.
- Exophoric links are links to items outside the text.
- Lexical chains are series of words that occur in the text and that have similar or related meanings.

6 Going beyond the text

Register

In this chapter, we will see how a text relates to, and in some sense is derived from, the context in which it is produced.

A text does not exist in a vacuum. It is created in a specific context, and it very much depends on that context. We can even say that it is determined by its context. If the context had been different in some way, then the text produced would also have been to some extent different. So, the context has a creative role in the production of text. But this is not a one-way process. The text once produced becomes a new element in the context, so its creation changes the context. So, there is a constant mutual causal process between context and text, each having an effect on the other.

Just as we can distinguish three metafunctions in a text, we can see three semiotic functions in the immediate context, which is frequently called the register. Each of these semiotic functions is directly related to one of the textual metafuctions. The semiotic function of field is related to the ideational metafunction; that of tenor is related to the interpersonal metafunction; and that of mode is related to the textual metafunction.

Field is the function of the immediate context that concerns the content of the discourse and the ongoing activity of which it is a part. There are some activities where the discourse is fairly incidental. For example, if the activity is a rugby match, then the discourse that occurs seems fairly marginal to the activity. One could almost, but perhaps not quite, imagine a game of rugby taking place without any language. Perhaps the only really essential bit of language would be the decisions of the referee, and although these would always be a form of language, it could be symbolic (whistling, pointing, etc.), rather than verbal. At the other end of the scale there are activities that are essentially language, such as a university lecture. In this case, the language is the main part of the activity and is essential to it. It is impossible to imagine a university lecture without language.

Tenor is concerned with the relationships set up between the protagonists in the discourse situation. These can be of two types: linguistic and social.

From the linguistic point of view, this will depend on the type of speech act taking place: questioner, replier, informer, or even doubter, advisor, and so on. Some of these roles may attempt to impose a role on another participant. For example, the role of questioner attempts to impose the role of replier on another participant, who, of course is free to refuse this role, by refusing to reply. The social roles involved will be determined by the relative social positions of the participants in the discourse in terms in the social situation in which they find themselves; typical relationships of this kind would be: shopkeeper–client; doctor–patient; teacher–learner; boss–employee; friend–friend. This may seem relatively straightforward, but some situations can be fairly complex. There are some television programmes, for example, where a politician, or other public figure, is interviewed by one, or more journalists, with a studio audience present, who can on occasion also intervene; in addition, there is the television audience at home, who frequently also have the option of intervening by telephone, e-mail or SMS. When the interviewee replies to a question, to whom is he replying? He presumably wishes to convince the viewers at home, but if he has not satisfied the journalists (or the studio audience), they might well come back at him with a supplementary question. Thus, the situation is complicated by his having to reply to a number of different interlocutors with each of whom he has a different social relationship.

Mode is the function that is concerned with the means or channels of communication. In its simplest form this means written discourse or oral discourse. However, there are many types of text that are more complex. The script of a film is written discourse, in the simplistic sense that it is printed on paper. But it is not primarily written to be read (except by the actor who learns it by heart). It is intended to be heard, as though it were oral discourse; so, listeners should hear it as a simulacre of oral discourse. When a priest reads the Gospel in church, the congregation hear the words spoken, but what they hear was intended to be read, so in this case we have written discourse that is rendered orally. The same sort of thing happens at a poetry reading with the added complication that many poets would say that poetry should be heard rather than read silently. There are some texts that are written to be read, but not linearly, that is from beginning to end; this is typical of reference works, like dictionaries and telephone directories.

Take for example the rules for the game of football. The field is the game of football itself and its organization. The tenor is the relationship between the games authorities (e.g. FIFA) and the players, officials, and administrators who are involved in the game. The mode is a text written to be read silently, though not necessarily linearly.

Consider the following text, which is an extract from a user's guide to a telephone printed in 2007 (*Guide d'utilisation Nokia 5200*, 2007).

Munissez-vous de votre carte USIM et suivez les étapes ci-dessous.

1. Détachez délicatement la carte USIM de son support en plastique. Ses connecteurs sont fragiles, évitez de les toucher en manipulant la carte.
2. Retirez le couvercle de la batterie en appuyant sur le taquet en haut du téléphone. Retirez la batterie.
3. Ouvrez le support en métal de la carte USIM en soulevant le loquet.
4. Placez la carte USIM dans son support de façon à ce qu'elle s'ajuste dans l'encadrement. Vérifiez que les contacts dorés de la carte sont tournés vers le bas. Refermez le support en appuyant dessus jusqu'à ce qu'il s'enclenche.

This text falls into the generic category of instructions for use, and this particular extract is concerned with the instructions for inserting a USIM card into a mobile telephone. This constitutes its field. The tenor is the relationship between the company (its designers, engineers, and sales staff), and the potential buyer of the phone before it is sold, and the actual buyer after it is sold. The mode is that of a written text intended to be read silently, and that must be read linearly, otherwise the steps in the instructions will not be in the correct order.

Some see the systemic functional model as a sort of Russian doll, with grammatical function at the centre surrounded by the three metafunctions; these in turn are surrounded by the semiotic functions of register. Some then see this as being surrounded by the wider context, or context of culture, and this in itself by ideology. However, there is a possible argument that would see ideology as being part of tenor at the level of register (Banks 2009b).

Summary of chapter 6

- Register deals with the functions of the immediate context.
- Register is analysed in terms of field, tenor, and mode.
- Field is the on-going activity of which the text is a part.
- Tenor is the relationship between those involved in the linguistic activity.
- Mode is the means by which the message is conveyed.

7 Moulding the text

Grammatical metaphor

In this chapter, we will see how the most usual ways of using language can be modified to give special effects in a text.

Language provides us with a set of resources that we use to encode the messages we wish to convey. Some of these resources are the normal or congruent ways of encoding our messages. For example, if we wish to express a process, the congruent way of doing so is to use a verb; if we wish to express an entity, whether it be physical or abstract, we would normally use a noun; if we wish to express the quality of an entity, the congruent way of doing so is to use an adjective, and so on. Thus, we can set up a series of congruent relationships:

Process → verb
Entity → noun
Quality → adjective

But language is not restricted to these congruent methods of encoding messages. We can use non-congruent means of expression by stepping outside these simple relationships. If we use a noun to express a process, that is we use a nominalized process, then this would be a non-congruent form; similarly, if we use a noun to express a quality, that is a nominalized quality, then that too would be a non-congruent form. Such non-congruent forms are known as grammatical metaphors. Grammatical metaphors are an exceedingly rich and powerful resource of the language. Consider the following example:

(94) Depuis maintenant plusieurs années, la **formation** en alternance se développe dans les universités.

(*Le Télégramme*, 17 septembre 2015)

The word *formation* is a noun, but it does not express an entity; it expresses a process, that of training or teaching, and is indeed derived from the verb *former*. So here, formation constitutes a nominalized process, and, as such, is a grammatical metaphor.

The following example is slightly different:

> (95) Les fleurs orange et jaune clair de la Suzanne aux yeux noirs (Thunbergia) sont de toute **beauté**.
>
> (*Le Télégramme*, 17 septembre 2015)

The word *beauté*, is, again, a noun, but it is not expressing an entity. Nor is it expressing a process; here it expresses a quality: its function is to describe the flower, and it is indeed derived from the adjective *beau*. This again is a grammatical metaphor.

Why should we use the term *metaphor* to describe this phenomenon? It seems very different to what has traditionally been called metaphor. Traditional metaphor, which is semantic and lexical in nature, is based on replacing a word, with another word of the same class but with a different meaning. So, when we say "the rosy fingers of the dawn" to mean "the rays of the sun at sunrise", the word *fingers* replaces the word *rays*. Both of these words are nouns, so a noun has replaced another noun, but they have different meanings. It is this curious mismatch that creates the metaphor that many people think of as a sort of poetic image. So, in traditional metaphor, a word of one class is replaced by another word of the same class, but with a different meaning. In grammatical metaphor, it is the other way round. We replace one word by a word from a different class, but that has the same basic meaning. *Formation* is a noun, and *former* is a verb, but they have the same basic meaning, that of training; *beauté* is a noun and *beau* is an adjective, but they have the same basic meaning of being beautiful. We can set this out in a simple diagram.

	form	meaning
traditional metaphor	same	different
grammatical metaphor	different	same

Since the type of grammatical metaphor that has received the most attention is that of nominalized processes, the rest of this section will deal with this type. What has been said so far might lead you to think that a nominalized process must be derived from a verb. Although most nominalized processes are derived from verbs, this is not absolutely necessary. The important point is that the nominalized form encodes a process rather than an entity.

The use of grammatical metaphor has two sorts of effect. The first of these is grammatical and syntactic and can further affect the way the text is structured. The second relates to meaning and how we conceive of it. The first type of effect is related to the fact that once a process is expressed in nominal form it has the grammatical features of nouns, so it can function as the subject or complement in a sentence, or as the nominal completive of a prepositional phrase. Moreover, since it now has nominal form, it can be modified or, more usually in French, qualified by, for example, adjectives and relative clauses.

> (96) La période de **plantation** idéale des clématites est à la fin de l'été.
> (*Le Télégramme*, 17 septembre 2015)

In this example, the nominalized process *plantation* functions as subject and is qualified by the adjective *idéale*, and by the prepositional phrase *des clématites*. Halliday (1988) has pointed out that in certain types of text, notably academic, this resource can be used to enhance the thematic progression. A process will be expressed in a congruent, non-metaphorical form in the rheme of a clause, and will then be taken up in metaphorical form as the theme of a following clause.

> (97) Par la suite, d'autres lecteurs, l'auteur de l'article ainsi que l'éditeur peuvent **réagir dans un va-et-vient incessant**, créant une sorte de polylogue hétéroclite et imprévisible. Cette **interaction** vive et intense a des retombées bénéfiques dans le débat sur les rapports entre la science et la société, sur la science et la découverte scientifique, mais aussi sur l'image que la revue de vulgarisation scientifique renvoie.
> (conference abstract, 2015)

In this example, part of the rheme of the first clause, comprising a process and its complement, *réagir dans un va-et-vient incessant*, is taken up in nominalized form as the theme of the following clause, *interaction*. Thus, grammatical metaphor is used in the thematic progression to help build up the argumentation of the text.

The second effect of nominalizing a process derives from the fact that a process is something that typically takes place and then it is over, while an entity is something that has a certain stability and permanence. When a process is nominalized it takes on some of the "feel" of an entity, and so we read it as being something more fixed and stable than it would have appeared expressed in verbal form. Presenting a process in nominal form is suggesting to the reader that this is something to be taken for granted. Halliday has said "you can argue with a clause but you can't argue with a nominal group" (Halliday & Martin 1993: 39). This trait has been extensively used in certain types of text, for example political (Banks 2013). Consider the following example.

(98) Les **affrontements** qui se déroulent dans différents quartiers populaire depuis plus d'une semaine, faisant vivre aux populations et aux salaries de ces quartiers des moments extrêmement difficiles, sont révélateurs des la **crise** sociale qui s'est développée : **pauvreté**, **chômage**, **précarisation** sociale généralisée, mais aussi **discriminations** et **relégation** sociale. Le **démantèlement** des **services** publics, l'**asphyxie** financière et le **mépris** des associations de terrain, l'**abandon** des politiques de **prévention** : tout cela est au cœur du **désarroi** qui s'exprime aujourd'hui. Quel avenir pour ces populations et leurs enfants ? Ces **violences** sont aussi les signes de l'**échec** des politiques répressives conçues comme seule **réponse** aux **questions** sociales.

(trade union tract, Rennes, 2005)

In this extract of 105 words, there are no less than 18 examples of grammatical metaphor (16 nominalized processes and two nominalised qualities). Thus, a message is being hammered home in a way that tends to prevent any argument.

There are some cases where grammatical metaphor can have an impact on other aspects of the text. Consider the following example.

(99) Il est vrai que le titulaire du perchoir a démarré dans la vie comme visiteur médical pour le compte d'un labo pharmaceutique.

(*Nouvel Observateur*, 12 décembre 2013)

What is the topical theme of this clause complex? Since there are two finite verbs, *est* and *a démarré*, we might be tempted to say that there are two clauses, a main clause with *Il* as its topical theme, and a subordinate clause with *le titulaire du perchoir* as its topical theme. It is difficult to claim that such a view would be false, but having *le titulaire du perchoir* simply as the internal theme of a subordinate clause probably does not correspond to our instinctive reading of the sentence. There is a further possibility that involves grammatical metaphor. If we consider that *Il est vrai que* is functoning as a grammatical metaphor of modality, that is it is the non-congruent encoding of something that in its congruent form would be an adverb expressing modality, like *certainement*, then we can say that *Il est vrai que* is functioning as the interpersonal theme, in which case *le titulaire du perchoir* becomes the main topical theme of the whole complex.

Even from this short and relatively simple description of grammatical metaphor, it can probably be realized that this is one of the most powerful resources available in the language.

Summary of chapter 7

- Grammatical metaphor is the use of a non-congruent form to encode a message.
- One of the commonest forms of grammatical metaphor is the encoding of a process in nominal rather than verbal form.

8 Expanding the interpersonal metafunction

Appraisal Theory

In this chapter, we will see how the interpersonal metafunction, which was introduced in Chapter 4, can be extended to bring out the ways in which the traces of the speaker, his feelings, and attitudes, can be seen to be present in the text.

There have been a number of extensions of the systemic functional approach and one of the most important of these has come to be known as Appraisal Theory (Martin & White 2005). Those who originally introduced this idea have pointed out that it is not a separate theory, and prefer not to use the word, "theory", but the term "Appraisal Theory" is commonly used. This is an attempt to work out in some detail the interpersonal aspect of language, in particular to see what the traces of the subjective presence of a speaker are in the text he produces. There are three basic systems of appraisal: attitude, engagement, and graduation.

8.1 Attitude

Attitude deals with the ways in which the feelings of the speaker are expressed in his text, and this can be further subdivided into three types: affect, judgement and appreciation. The first of these, affect, is concerned with emotion, and thus with the positive or negative feelings that we express towards events or objects around us.

> (100) Il y a deux ans, j'ai raté un concours que j'avais énormément préparé pour entrer dans une école de mode. Mon monde **s'est écroulé**, je n'avais aucun autre **désir**. Plutôt que de **me morfondre**, j'ai pris six mois sabbatiques pour voyager.
>
> (*Femme Actuelle*, 3–9 février 2014)

Within affect we can find such features as happiness, security, and satisfaction. Hence in this example, the feeling that the writer's whole world has collapsed (*s'est écroulé*), that she had no other desire (*désir*), and that she didn't mope about it (*se morfondre*) can be seen as entering into this system.

Judgement concerns that ways in which we express attitudes towards people and their behaviour, by admiring or criticizing, by praising or condemning them.

> (101) Il me tarde de le commencer ! J'ai lu presque tous ses livres. Elle fait partie de mes auteurs contemporains **préferés** ! Elle a une personnalité **incroyable** et son grain de folie me plaît.
>
> (*Fémina*, 22–28 septembre 2014)

In this short extract the adjectives *préférés* and *incroyable* can be seen as contributing to the system of judgement.

Appreciation is concerned with the ways in which we evaluate things.

> (102) Lausanne sans le Beau-Rivage, ce palace lourd Belle Epoque, posé au bord du lac Léman, face à un paysage alpin aussi **délectable** qu'une tablette de chocolat. Un des **plus belles** haltes d'Europe, vous diront les habitués. Depuis toujours. Depuis que cette bâtisse **mythique**, construite en 1861, a accueilli tout un panier garni de célébrités et politique, venus respirer l'air **pur** et rêver dans les lits king size des 168 chambres et suites.
>
> (*Nouvel Observateur*, 12 décembre 2013)

Here the words, *délectable*, *plus belle*, *mythique*, and, in this context, *pur*, can be seen as contributing to the appreciation of this extract.

Each of these three main functions can be broken down into more delicate functions. Affect can be seen in terms of positive and negative, while expressing such things as inclination, happiness, security, and satisfaction. Thus, in the following extract we can find examples of both positive and negative affect.

> (103) J'ai quatre enfants, alors les devoirs **j'en ai soupé**. J'ai souvent fini en leur **envoyant les cahiers à la figure**. . . Jusqu'à ce que j'aie la **bonne idée** de déléguer. Je dois avouer que moi-même, petite, je **n'aimais pas** faire mes devoirs, d'autant que mon père **s'énervait** beaucoup en les supervisant. Il y a des étudiants dans mon entourage, **ravis** de se faire ainsi en peu d'argent de poche. J'ai aussi un oncle très calé en maths qui aide beaucoup mon ainé. Cela **m'épargne** des **conflits** permanents et me permet **de profiter** un peu plus et mieux d'eux quand je rentre le soir.
>
> (*Marie France*, octobre 2015)

Among the positive markers, we could include *bonne idée, ravis, m'épargne*, and *de profiter*. The negative markers would include *j'en ai soupé, envoyant les cahiers à la figure, n'aimais pas, s'énervait*, and *conflits*, although it will be noted that here the negative effect of *conflits* is neutralized since it is the complement of *m'épargne*, and indeed the whole extract is about finding positive ways of overcoming the negative.

Judgement can be seen in terms of social esteem and social sanction, each of which can subsequently be broken down into positive and negative.

> (104) Gagnant de la Nouvelle Star en 2014, ce jeune Franco-Libanais affiche déjà, à 22 ans, **une vraie maturité** artistique. Il pratique une folk douce, en français et en anglais, menée par **le charme rêveur** de sa voix. Les arrangements ont du relief, s'autorisant le maximum (des **envolées lyriques**) et le minimum (une guitare seul), parfois dans une même chanson (*Poison, Dans l'espace*). On se sent bien dans cet album **détendu**, riche de nuances, qui parle avec **une bien-faisante fraicheur** du sentiment amoureux.
>
> (*Femme Actuelle*, 3–9 août 2015)

This extract can be seen as illustrating social esteem. Among the expressions that indicate this are *une vraie maturité, le charme rêveur, envolées lyriques, détendu*, and *une bien-faisante fraicheur*.

Appreciation can also be subdivided into positive and negative categories. Consider the following extract.

> (105) Sous l'**élégant** pseudonyme d'Elena Ferrante se cache une des plus **fascinantes** énigmes littéraires. La signora Ferrante est entrée dans la **clandestinité** littéraire dès son premier livre, il y a plus de vingt ans. Elle avait alors envoyé à son éditeur cet **avertissement** prémonitoire : "De tous vos écrivains, je serai celle qui vous importunera le moins. Je vous épargnerai jusqu'à ma présence." Comme Thomas Pynchon, autre romancier **fantôme**, Elena Ferrante n'a jamais dérogé à son vœu d'anonymat, **abandonnant** ses admirateurs à d'**incertaines déductions** : l'auteur serait de sexe féminin, né dans les années 1940 dans la région de Naples, qu'elle décrit si bien.
>
> (*Le Nouvel Observateur*, 14–20 janvier 2016)

A list of the positive markers of appreciation in this extract would include *élegant* and *fascinantes*, while the negative markers would include *clandestinité, avertissement, fantôme, abondonnant*, and *incertaines deductions*.

Many more distinctions can be made, taking the system to a high degree of delicacy, including the distinction between inscribed, explicit expression, and evoked, or implicit expression, but perhaps sufficient has been said here to show that this is a powerful tool in the systemic tradition for analysing texts.

8.2 Analysis of an authentic example

The following is an extract from the review of a production of a Shakespeare play (in French translation), which appeared in *Le Nouvel Observateur* 23 décembre 2015–6 janvier 2016.

> Sitôt nommé administrateur de la Comédie-Française, Eric Ruf annonçait qu'il mettrait sa carrière d'acteur entre parenthèses. Eu égard à son talent, c'est dommage. Par chance, il a reçu d'autres dons en partage. Son décor et sa mise en scène de "Peer Gynt", d'Ibsen, étaitent inoubliables. Ce que n'est pas ce "Roméo et Juliette" sage comme une image. Impersonnel. Frigide. Sans point de vue. Ruf le revendique d'ailleurs. Mais après avoir examiné une œuvre sous toutes ses coutures, ne faut-il pas choisir un angle d'attaque pour la mettre en scène ? Surtout s'il s'agit d'un classique archiconnu. Il n'y a rien de saillant dans ce spectacle. Tout y est fade.

The following, admittedly simple, analysis consists of listing the items that carry aspects of appraisal in the left-hand column, and categorizing them as affect, judgement or appreciation, and giving affect and appreciation in terms of positive or negative import, and judgement in terms of esteem or sanction.

Item	*Affect*	*Judgement*	*Appreciation*
entre parenthèses	negative		
talent		esteem	
dommage	negative		
chance	positive		
dons		esteem	
inoubliables			positive
sage comme une image			negative
impersonnel			negative

frigide			negative
sans point de vue			negative
ne faut-il pas	negative		
archiconnu		esteem	
rien de saillant			negative
fade			negative

Here it can be seen that the review starts off in the areas of affect and judgement, and where these are negative it is about Ruf's career, not this production of the play. The second part, however, is dominated by appreciation, and this is strongly negative, the only positive piece of appreciation relating to Ruf's prior production of *Pier Gynt*.

8.3 Engagement

Engagement deals with the extent to which a speaker accepts the content of his message as his own, or presents it in relation to other possible points of view. Where a message is a bald statement put forward as the point of view of the speaker, it is said to be monoglossic; where it takes into account the possibility of other opinions, either in favour or in opposition, it is said to be heteroglossic. Where it is heteroglossic, it is possible to distinguish between cases of disclaiming, proclaiming, entertaining, and attributing.

In disclaiming, the speaker presents himself as being opposed to some point of view by denying or countering it in some way.

> (106) Ne nous étonnons donc pas que les élèves s'interrogent sur l'utilité pratique d'un tel enseignement.
>
> (*Marianne*, 25–31 mai 2013)

By using the negative, the speaker sets himself in opposition to those who might be surprised, by saying that we should not be.

Proclaiming is more or less the opposite of this. It is where the speaker presents himself as approving of some supposed view.

> (107) C'est vrai que je ne peux pas supporter de ne pas être en train d'écrire.
>
> (*Le Nouvel Observateur*, 11 septembre 2014)

The phrase *C'est vrai que* aligns the speaker with a (real or supposed) previously expressed opinion.

In entertaining, the speaker accepts the possibility of a certain point of view. In the following example *Il me semble que* presents something as being possible, without claiming that it is actually the case.

(108) Il me semble que l'angoisse de vieillir chez la femme de 50 ans est moins forte.

(*Femme Actuelle*, 3–9 février 2014)

In attributing, the speaker presents something as being the opinion of others, but not necessarily his own. Thus, in the following example, something is presented as being a rumour, and so he is not claiming that it is true.

(109) La rumeur dit que, lors des fêtes de fin d'année, l'acteur aurait présenté sa belle à sa maman.

(*Femme Actuelle*, 3–9 février 2014)

8.4 Graduation

Graduation deals with the ways in which we grade our feelings or attitudes. There are two ways in which this can be done. Focus is the degree to which we say something is prototypical or not. Force is the degree to which we say something is strong or weak.

(110) Ainsi il est littéralement le premier – avec "Scorpio Rising" – à se servir de *pop songs*, de rock, pour illustrer ses images.

(*Le Nouvel Observateur*, 14 août 2014)

In this example, it is the word *littéralement* that emphasizes the uniqueness of being the first. This is an example of focus. The following is an example of force, where the word *indispensable* intensifies *condition.*

(111) La laïcité est une condition indispensable de la diversité culturelle.

(*Ouest France*, 9 août 2016)

Summary of chapter 8

- Appraisal deals with the ways in which the subjective presence of the speaker is present in the text.
- Attitude deals with the feelings of the speaker in terms of affect, judgement, and appreciation.
- Affect deals with the expression of the speaker's emotions.

- Judgement deals with the expression of the speaker's attitudes towards other people and their behaviour.
- Appreciation deals with how the speaker evaluates things.
- Engagement deals with how a speaker presents something as being his own opinion (monoglossic) or as deriving from some other source (heteroglossic).
- Graduation deals with how speakers grade things.

9 Signing off, but not closing down

In this short book, I have used textual analysis as a way of illustrating the various points that I wished to make. This may give the impression that Systemic Functional Linguistics is basically a framework for analysing texts. Although textual analysis is one of its uses, the theory is much more than that. It is a complete theory of language, and can be, and has been, used for language description, in diachronic and historical linguistics, for language learning, both mother tongue and foreign, and language for specific purposes, in translation studies, language pathology, computational linguistics, forensic linguistics, and so on.

In this book we have seen how the structural elements of French function together, to constitute the basic forms through which we encode meaning. We have seen how the meaning itself functions in three different ways: ideational, to describe the world around and within us; interpersonal, to express our attitudes to what we say and to those we communicate with; and textual, to order our discourse into meaningful communication. We have seen how language is not something isolated but is part of our social fabric, and is created by that social environment, without which it cannot truly be understood. We have seen how the immediate environment can be seen in terms of field, tenor, and mode. We have also looked at how language can be manipulated with grammatical metaphor, and how the interpersonal metafunction can be extended with Appraisal Theory.

I have made this book as short and as simple as I thought was possible. I hope that this will have given beginning students and those that new to this field an opportunity to enter this amazing area of study, which is what language is, and in this case, the French language in particular. However, because the book is intentionally simple, there is much that it does not say, and many complications have been glossed over. Because of that, this book should not be considered an end in itself. It is my hope that this book will have given the reader a taste for this subject, which will make him want to go further, to look at the theory in greater depth, and in greater detail, and since so little work has been done on the French language, to apply it to French. For that reason, the reader will find a list of books for suggested reading in the pages that follow.

I would also like to think that I have been able to communicate to the reader that fascination with language, with which I began this book, for, indeed, language is a fascinating phenomenon.

Further reading

There are very few books that deal specifically with French. The only book to date that attempts to present a Systemic Functional grammar of French is the following. Although ostensibly intended for students, it requires rather more familiarity with the theory than the present book.

Caffarel, Alice (2006): *A Systemic Functional Grammar of French, from Grammar to Discourse*, London, Continuum.

There are two books of articles dealing with French. Of the eight articles in the first book, five are written in French and three in English. The second has two items written in French and four in English.

Banks, David, Simon Eason & Janet Ormrod (eds.) (2009): *La linguistique systémique fonctionnelle et la langue française*, Paris, L'Harmattan.

Banks, David & Janet Ormrod (eds.) (2016): *Nouvelles études sur le transitivité en français. Une perspective systémique fonctionnelle*, Paris, L'Harmattan.

There is one presentation of the theory that deals with English but is written in French.

Banks, David (2005): *Introduction à la linguistique systémique fonctionnelle de l'anglais*, Paris, L'Harmattan.

Almost all other books in this field deal basically with English. The fundamental book that all others in Systemic Functional Linguistics refer to is Halliday's *Introduction to Functional Grammar*. Originally published in 1984, this has gone through several editions, the most recent being the 4th edition in 2014.

Halliday, M.A.K. (rev. by Christian M.I.M. Matthiessen) (2014): *Halliday's Introduction to Functional Grammar*, 4th edn., Abingdon, Routledge.

Before going to this, some may prefer to look at a simpler introduction (though none are as simple as the present book). The earliest of these is by Margaret Berry, published in two small volumes; although many might think this now out of date, I feel it still has much to be said for it.

Berry, Margaret (1975): *Introduction to Systemic Linguistics, Vol. 1 Structure and Systèms*, London, Batsford.

Berry, Margaret (1977): *Introduction to Systemic Linguistics, Vol. 2 Levels and Links*, London, Batsford.

These two volumes were reprinted by the Department of English Studies at the University of Nottingham in 1991. Other introductions would include the following.

Bloor, Thomas & Meriel Bloor (2004): *The Functional Analysis of English: A Hallidayan Approach*, 2nd edn., London, Arnold.
Eggins, Suzanne (1994): *An Introduction to Systemic Functional Linguistics*, London, Pinter.
Lock, Graham (1996): *Functional English Grammar: An Introduction for Second Language Teachers*, Cambridge, Cambridge University Press.
Thompson, Geoff (2004): *Introducing Functional Grammar*, 2nd edn., London, Arnold.

Some books for students include exercises.

Downing, Angela & Philip Locke (2006): *English Grammar: A University Course*, Abingdon, Routledge.
Martin, J.R., Christian M.I.M. Matthiessen & Clare Painter (1997): *Working with Functional Grammar*, London, Arnold.

Halliday has himself written numerous other books, sometimes single-handedly, sometimes with a co-author. Many of these have become classics. In general, these are more difficult than the books written for a student readership. The following is a small selection;

Halliday, M.A.K. (1973): *Explorations in the Functions of Language*, London, Arnold.
Halliday, M.A.K. (1975): *Learning How to Mean – Explorations in the Development of Language*, London, Arnold.
Halliday, M.A.K. (1978): *Language as Social Semiotic: The Social Interpretation of Language and Meaning*, London, Arnold.
Halliday, M.A.K. (1989): *Spoken and Written Language*, 2nd edn., Oxford, Oxford University Press.
Halliday, M.A.K. & J.R. Martin (1993): *Writing Science, Literacy and Discursive Power*, London, Falmer Press.
Halliday, M.A.K. & Christian M.I.M. Matthiessen (1999): *Construing Experience through Meaning: A Language-Based Approach to Cognition*, London, Cassell.
Halliday, M.A.K. & William S. Greaves (2008): *Intonation in the Grammar of English*, London, Equinox.
Halliday, M.A.K. & Jonathan J. Webster (2014): *Text Linguistics: The How and Why of Meaning*, Sheffield, Equinox.

The numerous articles that Halliday has written have been collected, and are published as his Collected Works by Bloomsbury Publishing. There are now 11 volumes.

The following are general, but highly detailed accounts:

Martin, J.R. (1992): *English Text, System and Structure*, Amsterdam, John Benjamins.

Matthiessen, Christian (1995): *Lexicogrammatical Cartography: English Systems*, Tokyo, International Language Sciences.

The following is a useful listing of technical terms in systemic functional linguistics, with definitions and explanations:

Matthiessen, Christian M.I.M., Kazuhiro Teruya & Marvin Lam (2010): *Key Terms in Systemic Functional Linguistics*, London, Continuum.

Among the many books dealing with more specific topics, one might cite the following.

Cummings, Michael (2010): *An Introduction to the Grammar of Old English, a Systemic Functional Approach*, London, Equinox.
Lewin, Beverly A., Jonathan Fine & Lynne Young (2001): *Expository Discourse: A Genre-Based Approach to Social Science Research Texts*, London, Continuum.
Martin, J.R. & David Rose (2008): *Genre Relations: Mapping Culture*, London, Equinox.
Martin, J.R. & P.R.R. White (2005): *The Language of Evaluation: Appraisal in English*, Basingstoke, Palgrave Macmillan.
Morley, G. David (2000): *Syntax in Functional Grammar: An Introduction to Lexicogrammar in Systemic Linguistics*, London, Continuum.
O'Halloran, Kay L. (2005): *Mathematical Discourse: Language, Symbolism and Visual Images*, London, Continuum.
Tench, Paul (1996): *The Intonation Systems of English*, London, Cassell.
Tucker, Gordon H. (1998): *The Lexicogrammar of Adjectives: A Systemic Functional Approach to Lexis*, London, Cassell.

Finally, the following is a small selection of collections of articles, on various topics.

Banks, David (ed.) (2004): *Text and Texture: Systemic Functional Viewpoints on the Nature and Structure of Text*, Paris, L'Harmattan.
Bowcher, Wendy L. & Bradley A. Smith (eds.) (2014): *Systemic Phonoogy: Rencent Studies in English*, Sheffield, Equinox.
Fries, Peter H., Michael Cummings, David Lockwood & William Spruiell (eds.) (2002): *Relations and Functions within and around Language*, London, Continuum.
Fontaine, Lise, Tom Bartlett & Gerard O'Grady (eds.) (2013): *Systemic Functional Linguistics: Exploring Choices*, Cambridge, Cambridge University Press.
Ghadessy, Mohsen (ed.) (1988): *Registers of Written English, Situational Factors and Linguistic Features*, London, Pinter.
Hasan, Ruqaiya & Peter H. Fries (eds.) (1995): *On Subject and Theme, a Discourse Functional Perspective*, Amsterdam, John Benjamins.
Hasan, Ruqaiya, Christian Matthiessen & Jonathan J. Webster (eds.) (2007): *Continuing Discourse on Language: A Functional Perspective*, 2 vols., London, Equinox.
Martin, J.R. & Robert Veel (eds.) (1998): *Reading Science: Critical and Functional Perspectives on Discourses of Science*, London, Routledge.

Miller, Donna R. & Paul Bayley (eds.) (2016): *Hybridity in Systemic Functional Linguistics: Grammar, Text and Discursive Context*, Sheffield, Equinox.

O'Grady, Gerard, Tom Bartlett & Lise Fontaine (eds.) (2013): *Choice in Language: Applications in Text Analysis*, Sheffield, Equinox.

Starc, Sonja, Carys Jones & Arianna Maiorani (eds.) (2015): *Meaning Making in Text: Multimomdal and Multilingual Functional Perspectives*, Basingstoke, Palgrave Macmillan.

Swain, Elizabeth (ed.) (2010): *Thresholds and Potentialities of Systemic Fucntional Linguistics: Mulitlingual, Multimodal and Other Specialized Discourses*, Trieste, Edizioni Università di Trieste.

Ventola, Eija & Anna Mauranen (eds.) (1996): *Academic Writing: Intercultural and Textual Issues*, Amsterdam, John Benjamins.

English–French glossary

The following glossary includes terms used in this book with their French equivalents and also many other terms that readers are likely to find in the books listed in the Suggested Reading. I am indebted to Jacques François for terms relating to Appraisal Theory.

The English term is given on the left and its French equivalent on the right. This is followed by a brief note giving the basic meaning of the term. Since these notes are necessarily very short, they do not have all the precision a full definition would require.

<table>
<tr><td>α-clause</td><td>Proposition α</td></tr>
<tr><td colspan="2">An α-clause is a main or coordinate clause in a clause complex.</td></tr>
<tr><td>Actor</td><td>Acteur</td></tr>
<tr><td colspan="2">The actor is a participant in a material process. It is the conscious instigator of the process.</td></tr>
<tr><td>Adjunct</td><td>Ajout</td></tr>
<tr><td colspan="2">The main type of adjunct is the circumstantial adjunct. This is the constituent that gives the circumstances (where, when, how, etc.) of the clause. Other types of adjunct are the textual adjunct that links the clause to the rest of the text and the interpersonal adjunct that gives the attitude of the speaker.</td></tr>
<tr><td>Affect</td><td>Affect</td></tr>
<tr><td colspan="2">In appraisal, affect is that part of attitude that deals with emotions and feelings.</td></tr>
<tr><td>Affected</td><td>Affecté</td></tr>
<tr><td colspan="2">The affected is the participant in a material process that is modified in some way by the process.</td></tr>
<tr><td>Agent</td><td>Agent</td></tr>
<tr><td colspan="2">The agent is a causal element in a process. It can be actor, force or instrument.</td></tr>
<tr><td>Appraisal</td><td>Evaluation</td></tr>
</table>

<table>
<tr><td colspan="2">Appraisal (Theory) is an attempt to provide a framework for analysing the traces of the subjective presence of the speaker in the text.</td></tr>
<tr><td>Appreciation</td><td>Appréciation</td></tr>
<tr><td colspan="2">In appraisal, appreciation is that part of attitude that deals with the ways in which the speaker evaluates things.</td></tr>
<tr><td>Attribute</td><td>Attribut</td></tr>
<tr><td colspan="2">The attribute is the participant in an attributive relational process that gives a characteristic of the first participant, the carrier.</td></tr>
<tr><td>Attributive relational process</td><td>Procès relationnel attributif</td></tr>
<tr><td colspan="2">An attributive relational process states the relationship between an entity, called the carrier, and one of its features or characteristics, called the attribute.</td></tr>
<tr><td>Attitude</td><td>Attitude</td></tr>
<tr><td colspan="2">Attitude is a function in appraisal that deals with the ways in which the feelings of the speaker are expressed in his text.</td></tr>
<tr><td>Auxiliary</td><td>Auxiliaire</td></tr>
<tr><td colspan="2">The auxiliary is a component of the verbal group and is placed before the verb. It can express modality, voice, or aspect.</td></tr>
<tr><td>β-clause</td><td>Proposition β</td></tr>
<tr><td colspan="2">A β-clause is a dependant clause which has not been rankshifted.</td></tr>
<tr><td>Behaver</td><td>Réactif</td></tr>
<tr><td colspan="2">For linguists who use the category of behavioural process, the single participant in this process is a behaver.</td></tr>
<tr><td>Behavioural process</td><td>Procès réactionnel</td></tr>
<tr><td colspan="2">Behavioural process is a process type used by many linguists to indicate a process that is said to be on the borderline between material and mental process.</td></tr>
<tr><td>Beneficiary</td><td>Bénéficiaire</td></tr>
<tr><td colspan="2">A beneficiary is a participant in a material clause on behalf of whom the process is carried out.</td></tr>
<tr><td>Carrier</td><td>Porteur</td></tr>
<tr><td colspan="2">A carrier is the participant in an attributive relational clause; it is the participant of whom something is attributed.</td></tr>
<tr><td>Classifier</td><td>Classifieur</td></tr>
<tr><td colspan="2">A classifier is a type of modifier that places the head in a class or category; usually it is not gradable.</td></tr>
<tr><td>Clause</td><td>Proposition</td></tr>
<tr><td colspan="2">A clause is the basic unit of a text. It is made up of a predicator, may have one or two participants (occasionally three), and may also have circumstances.</td></tr>
</table>

<table>
<tr><td>Clause complex</td><td>Complèxe propositionnel</td></tr>
<tr><td colspan="2">A clause complex is a unit made up of more than one clause. It corresponds to a sentence in most other approaches.</td></tr>
<tr><td>Client</td><td>Bénéficière</td></tr>
<tr><td colspan="2">Client is used by some linguists as an alternative to beneficiary.</td></tr>
<tr><td>Cohesion</td><td>Cohésion</td></tr>
<tr><td colspan="2">Cohesion is the set of linguistic resources used to make a text into a coherent whole.</td></tr>
<tr><td>Collocation</td><td>Collocation</td></tr>
<tr><td colspan="2">Collocation refers to the co-occurrence of two (or more) words in texts.</td></tr>
<tr><td>Comment adjunct</td><td>Ajout d'attitude</td></tr>
<tr><td colspan="2">A comment adjunct is an interpersonal adjunct that expresses the attitude of the speaker.</td></tr>
<tr><td>Complement</td><td>Complément</td></tr>
<tr><td colspan="2">The complement is a main constituent of the clause. It is the second participant in the clause.</td></tr>
<tr><td>Completive</td><td>Complétif</td></tr>
<tr><td colspan="2">A completive is the grammatical function of a nominal group that follows a preposition with which it constitutes a prepositional phrase.</td></tr>
<tr><td>Conflation</td><td>Assimilation</td></tr>
<tr><td colspan="2">Conflation is the combination of two separate items, as when two separate analyses of a single clause are combined to give a fuller picture.</td></tr>
<tr><td>Congruent wording</td><td>Encodage non marqué</td></tr>
<tr><td colspan="2">The congruent wording is the most usual way of encoding or expressing something in words.</td></tr>
<tr><td>Conjunction</td><td>Conjonction</td></tr>
<tr><td colspan="2">A conjunction is a word that links two linguistic elements.</td></tr>
<tr><td>Conjunctive adjunct</td><td>Ajout conjonctif</td></tr>
<tr><td colspan="2">A conjunctive adjunct is an adjunct whose function is to link the clause to the rest of the discourse.</td></tr>
<tr><td>Context</td><td>Contexte</td></tr>
<tr><td colspan="2">The context refers to the social situation in which a text is produced.</td></tr>
<tr><td>Contingency</td><td>Circonstances contingentes</td></tr>
<tr><td colspan="2">Contingency is a type of circumstance expressing a condition or concession.</td></tr>
<tr><td>Deictic</td><td>Déictique</td></tr>
<tr><td colspan="2">A deictic is a word that refers to another element in the discourse.</td></tr>
<tr><td>Delicacy</td><td>Finesse</td></tr>
</table>

Delicacy refers to the degree or level of detail that has been achieved in a system network.	
Determiner	Déterminant
A determiner is a word in a nominal group whose function is to identify or distinguish the head.	
Disjunct	Ajout d'attitude
A disjunct is a type of adjunct that gives the attitude of the speaker.	
Elaboration	Elaboration
Elaboration is a method of expanding a clause by adding a restatement, clarification, or example.	
Ellipsis	Ellipse
Ellipsis is the omission of a word that can be understood from the surrounding discourse.	
Embedded clause	Proposition enchâssée
An embedded clause is a clause that is not a main or coordinate clause, and forms a part of a clause complex.	
Embedding	Enchâssement
Embedding is the insertion of a clause with a dependant function in a clause complex.	
Enhancement	Embellissement
Enhancement is a method of expanding a clause by adding qualifications such as time, place, cause, or condition.	
Engagement	Engagement
Engagement is a category within appraisal whereby a speaker accepts the content of his message as his own (monoglossic) or in relation to other points of view (heteroglossic).	
Epithet	Epithète
An epithet is a modifier in a nominal group. It is qualitative, so describes but does not classify the head.	
Ergativity	Ergativité
Ergativity is an alternative to transitivity as a method of analysing the structure of the clause. This basically involves a process and an entity, known as the medium, that is essential for the process to take place.	
Event	Evénement
An event is an occurrence of a physical nature, and a type of material process.	
Evoked	Implicite
In appraisal, an evoked function is one that is implicit.	
Existent	Existant

The existent is the entity that is said to exist in a clause of existential process.	
Existential process	Procès existentiel
An existential process is one that states the existence of an entity.	
Expansion	Expansion
Expansion is a method of elaborating, extending or enhancing a clause by adding a dependant clause.	
Experiencer	Ressenteur
Experiencer is sometimes used as an alternative to senser for the conscious entity who experiences a mental process.	
Experiential	Expérientiel
Experiential is that part of the ideational metafunction that deals with the relationship between a process and its associated participants and circumstances.	
Extension	Extension
An extension is a word in a verbal group that follows the verb and is an essential part of its meaning.	
Extent	Etendu
Extent is a type of circumstance that expresses duration in time or extension in space.	
Field	Champ
Field is a function of register. It relates to the ongoing activity of which the text under consideration is a part.	
Finite	Conjugue
The finite is that part of the verbal group that is used to indicate aspect, modality, voice, or mood.	
Focalized	Focalisé
The focalized is the component of the tone group that carries the tonic accent. It is frequently called the new.	
Force	Force
Force is a participant in a material process. It is the non-conscious instigator of the process. In appraisal, the term "force" is also used for the type of graduation that indicates the extent to which something said is strong or weak.	
Functional	Fonctionnel
Functional, as applied to language, refers to the ways in which the language works. This can be internal: the ways in which the parts of the language work together to create meaning; or external: the ways in which the language works in society to create meaning.	
Generic structure potential	Structure générique puissancielle
Generic structure potential is the set of possible structures of a particular situation.	

<table>
<tr><td>Given</td><td>Donnée</td></tr>
<tr><td colspan="2">Given is a component of information structure. It is the element that the speaker presents as being already available to his addressees.</td></tr>
<tr><td>Goal</td><td>Affecté</td></tr>
<tr><td colspan="2">Goal is an alternative to affected. It is the participant that is modified in some way by the process.</td></tr>
<tr><td>Graduation</td><td>Graduation</td></tr>
<tr><td colspan="2">In appraisal, graduation refers to the ways in which the speaker grades his attitudes and feelings.</td></tr>
<tr><td>Grammatical metaphor</td><td>Métaphore grammaticale</td></tr>
<tr><td colspan="2">Grammatical metaphor is the use of a non-congruent means of expression.</td></tr>
<tr><td>Group</td><td>Groupe</td></tr>
<tr><td colspan="2">A group is a major constituent of the clause.</td></tr>
<tr><td>Happiness</td><td>Bonheur</td></tr>
<tr><td colspan="2">Happiness is a feature of affect in appraisal.</td></tr>
<tr><td>Head</td><td>Tête</td></tr>
<tr><td colspan="2">The head is the central and obligatory word in a nominal group.</td></tr>
<tr><td>Headword</td><td>Tête</td></tr>
<tr><td colspan="2">Headword is an alternative to head.</td></tr>
<tr><td>Hypotaxis</td><td>Hypotaxe</td></tr>
<tr><td colspan="2">Hypotaxis is the combination of elements of unequal status.</td></tr>
<tr><td>Ideational metafunction</td><td>Métafonction idéationnelle</td></tr>
<tr><td colspan="2">The ideational metafunction is the level of meaning that represents the external physical world or the internal world of our thoughts and feelings.</td></tr>
<tr><td>Ideational theme</td><td>Thème idéationnel</td></tr>
<tr><td colspan="2">Ideational theme is an alternative term for topical theme. In English, it is the first main component (subject, circumstantial adjunct, complement, or predicator) in the clause, and represents the speaker's starting point.</td></tr>
<tr><td>Identifying</td><td>Identifiant</td></tr>
<tr><td colspan="2">Identifying is the type of relational process that relates two expressions that have the same referent.</td></tr>
<tr><td>Inclination</td><td>Penchant</td></tr>
<tr><td colspan="2">Inclination is a feature of affect in appraisal.</td></tr>
<tr><td>Information structure</td><td>Structure informationnelle</td></tr>
<tr><td colspan="2">Information structure is the structure of a tone group. It distinguishes between a given and a focalized (or new).</td></tr>
<tr><td>Inscribed</td><td>Expicite</td></tr>
</table>

<table>
<tr><td colspan="2">In appraisal, an inscribed function is one that is explicit.</td></tr>
<tr><td>Instantiation</td><td>Actualisation</td></tr>
<tr><td colspan="2">Instantiation is the way in which the potential of the language system is made concrete in an actual text.</td></tr>
<tr><td>Instrument</td><td>Instrument</td></tr>
<tr><td colspan="2">The instrument is a participant in a material process. It is a causal element of the process, but requires a named or unnamed conscious agent in order to act.</td></tr>
<tr><td>Interpersonal metafunction</td><td>Métafonction interpersonelle</td></tr>
<tr><td colspan="2">The interpersonal metafunction is the level of meaning that relates to the relationships established by the speaker with his addressees or with his message.</td></tr>
<tr><td>Interpersonal theme</td><td>Thème interpersonel</td></tr>
<tr><td colspan="2">An interpersonal theme is a non-obligatory theme that indicates the attitude of the speaker.</td></tr>
<tr><td>Judgement</td><td>Jugement</td></tr>
<tr><td colspan="2">In appraisal, judgement is a function of attitude indicating how the speaker feels towards people and their behaviour.</td></tr>
<tr><td>Lexicogrammar</td><td>Lexicogrammaire</td></tr>
<tr><td colspan="2">Lexicogrammar is that level of language that deals with grammatical function and lexis.</td></tr>
<tr><td>Location</td><td>Localisation</td></tr>
<tr><td colspan="2">Location is a circumstance that locates a clause in space or time.</td></tr>
<tr><td>Locution</td><td>Discours</td></tr>
<tr><td colspan="2">A locution is a projection (direct or indirect speech) that gives the words spoken (direct) or a report of them (indirect).</td></tr>
<tr><td>Logical</td><td>Logique</td></tr>
<tr><td colspan="2">The logical function is a component of the ideational metafunction. It concerns the ways in which different elements are linked together.</td></tr>
<tr><td>Logical grammatical metaphor</td><td>Métaphore grammaticale logique</td></tr>
<tr><td colspan="2">A logical grammatical metaphor is the non-congruent expression of a logical function link.</td></tr>
<tr><td>Manner</td><td>Manière</td></tr>
<tr><td colspan="2">Manner is a circumstance expressing the way in which a process takes place.</td></tr>
<tr><td>Material process</td><td>Procès matériel</td></tr>
<tr><td colspan="2">A material process is an action or event of a physical nature.</td></tr>
<tr><td>Matter</td><td>Propos</td></tr>
<tr><td colspan="2">Matter is a circumstance that states the topic of speech or thought.</td></tr>
<tr><td>Medium</td><td>Moyen</td></tr>
</table>

<table>
<tr><td colspan="2">The medium is a participant in the ergative analysis of a clause. It is the participant that is essential for the process to take place.</td></tr>
<tr><td>Mental process</td><td>Procès mental</td></tr>
<tr><td colspan="2">A mental process is an event of a cerebral nature. It can be cognitive, affective, or perceptive.</td></tr>
<tr><td>Metafunction</td><td>Métafonction</td></tr>
<tr><td colspan="2">A metafunction is one of the three main levels of meaning: ideational, the representation of the world, interpersonal, the relationships established by the speaker, and textual, the way the message is organized.</td></tr>
<tr><td>Modal adjunct</td><td>Ajout de modalité</td></tr>
<tr><td colspan="2">A modal adjunct is an adjunct that expresses the attitude of the speaker.</td></tr>
<tr><td>Modality</td><td>Modalité</td></tr>
<tr><td colspan="2">Modality is the expression of the speaker's judgement of the validity of a proposition, or his attribution of obligation or permission.</td></tr>
<tr><td>Mode</td><td>Mode</td></tr>
<tr><td colspan="2">Mode is a function of register. It refers to the way in which a message is communicated, basically, written or spoken.</td></tr>
<tr><td>Modifier</td><td>Modifieur</td></tr>
<tr><td colspan="2">A modifier is a word to the left of the head that gives extra information about the head.</td></tr>
<tr><td>Mood</td><td>Mode</td></tr>
<tr><td colspan="2">Mood is expressed within the interpersonal metafunction. It is the basic orientation of the clause as declarative, interrogative, or imperative. The word is also frequently used as an abbreviation of mood element, which is a component of the interpersonal metafunction and is made up of the subject and finite.</td></tr>
<tr><td>Mood adjunct</td><td>Ajout de mode</td></tr>
<tr><td colspan="2">A mood adjunct is an adjunct that expresses the attitude of the speaker.</td></tr>
<tr><td>Negative</td><td>Négatif</td></tr>
<tr><td colspan="2">Negative is one of the poles of the polarity system, the other being positive.</td></tr>
<tr><td>Negotiation</td><td>Négotiation</td></tr>
<tr><td colspan="2">Negotiation is constituent of the interpersonal metafunction, and analyses the clause in terms of a negotiator and remainder. This is an alternative to an analysis in terms of mood (element) and residue.</td></tr>
<tr><td>Network</td><td>Réseau</td></tr>
<tr><td colspan="2">A network is the system formed by a series of choices representing the resources of a language.</td></tr>
<tr><td>New</td><td>Nouvelle</td></tr>
<tr><td colspan="2">The new is an alternative term for focalized. It is the part of a tone unit identified by the tonic accent.</td></tr>
<tr><td>Numerative</td><td>Quantifieur</td></tr>
</table>

<table>
<tr><td colspan="2">A numerative is a modifier that quantifies the head.</td></tr>
<tr><td>Operator</td><td>Opérateur</td></tr>
<tr><td colspan="2">The operator is the word that encodes the finite.</td></tr>
<tr><td>Parataxis</td><td>Parataxe</td></tr>
<tr><td colspan="2">Parataxis is the relationship between elements of equal status.</td></tr>
<tr><td>Phenomenon</td><td>Phénomène</td></tr>
<tr><td colspan="2">The phenomenon is a participant in a mental process, and expresses the content of the experience.</td></tr>
<tr><td>Participant</td><td>Participant</td></tr>
<tr><td colspan="2">A participant is an element that takes part in a process.</td></tr>
<tr><td>Phonology</td><td>Phonologie</td></tr>
<tr><td colspan="2">Phonology is the study of language in terms of sound.</td></tr>
<tr><td>Polarity</td><td>Polarité</td></tr>
<tr><td colspan="2">Polarity is the system that distinguishes between positive and negative.</td></tr>
<tr><td>Positive</td><td>Positif</td></tr>
<tr><td colspan="2">Positive is one of the poles of the system of polarity, the other being negative.</td></tr>
<tr><td>Possessed</td><td>Possession</td></tr>
<tr><td colspan="2">The possessed is a participant in a possessive relational process. It is in some way included in the possessor, typically as a possession.</td></tr>
<tr><td>Possessor</td><td>Possesseur</td></tr>
<tr><td colspan="2">The possessor is a participant in a possessive relational process. It is the participant that possesses or in some way includes the possessed.</td></tr>
<tr><td>Predicator</td><td>Prédicateur</td></tr>
<tr><td colspan="2">The predicator is the group that encodes the process.</td></tr>
<tr><td>Preposition</td><td>Préposition</td></tr>
<tr><td colspan="2">A preposition is the word that introduces a prepositional phrase, and precedes a nominal group known as the completive.</td></tr>
<tr><td>Process</td><td>Procès</td></tr>
<tr><td colspan="2">A process is the action, event, or state that forms the central element in a clause.</td></tr>
<tr><td>Projection</td><td>Projection</td></tr>
<tr><td colspan="2">Projection is a feature of the logical function whereby speech or thought (direct or indirect) is expressed.</td></tr>
<tr><td>Qualifier</td><td>Qualifieur</td></tr>
<tr><td colspan="2">A qualifier is an element at the rank of word that follows the head and gives extra information about it.</td></tr>
<tr><td>Quality</td><td>Qualité</td></tr>
</table>

Quality is a circumstance expressing the way in which the process takes place.	
Range	Portée
Range is a participant in a material process. It expresses the extent of the process, or is a re-expression of the process itself. Some books use scope instead of range and use range for the equivalent participant in an ergative analysis.	
Rank	Rang
A rank is a level of the system of grammatical functions such as clause, group or word.	
Rankshift	Enchassement
Rankshift is the resource that enables a unit of one rank to function at a different rank.	
Realization	Réalisation
Realization is the way in which a choice in a systemic network is carried out.	
Receiver	Recepteur
A receiver is a participant in a material or verbal process towards whom the process is directed.	
Recipient	Recepteur
Recipient is an alternative term for receiver, the participant in a material or verbal process towards whom the process is directed.	
Reference	Référence
Reference is the way in which an element in a text can refer to other items in the text or in the external world.	
Register	Registre
Register is a function of context and is analysed in terms of field, tenor, and mode.	
Relational process	Procès relationnel
A relational process is a process that links two entities or an entity with one of its characteristics.	
Residue	Reste
Residue is part of the mood structure of the clause. It is that part that is not included in the mood element.	
Rheme	Rhème
Rheme is part of the thematic structure of the clause. It is that part that is not included in the theme.	
Satisfaction	Satisfaction
In appraisal, satisfaction is a function of affect.	
Sayer	Annonceur
The sayer is a participant in a verbal process. It is the participant who is communicating something.	
Scale	Echelle

<table>
<tr><td colspan="2">Scale is made up of the different ranks, realisation and delicacy.</td></tr>
<tr><td>Security</td><td>Sécurité</td></tr>
<tr><td colspan="2">In appraisal, security is a function of affect.</td></tr>
<tr><td>Senser</td><td>Ressenteur</td></tr>
<tr><td colspan="2">The senser is a participant in a mental clause. It is the participant who is undergoing an experience.</td></tr>
<tr><td>Social esteem</td><td>Estime sociale</td></tr>
<tr><td colspan="2">In appraisal, social esteem is a function of judgement.</td></tr>
<tr><td>Social sanction</td><td>Sanction sociale</td></tr>
<tr><td colspan="2">In appraisal, social sanction is a function of judgement.</td></tr>
<tr><td>Speech function</td><td>Fonction discursive</td></tr>
<tr><td colspan="2">In the interpersonal metafunction, a speech function is one of the combinations given by the functions of giving or requesting information or goods and services.</td></tr>
<tr><td>Stratum</td><td>Strate</td></tr>
<tr><td colspan="2">Strata are the general levels of language such as semantics, lexicogrammar, and phonology.</td></tr>
<tr><td>Subject</td><td>Sujet</td></tr>
<tr><td colspan="2">The subject is a group and a constituent (the first participant) of a clause.</td></tr>
<tr><td>Substitution</td><td>Substitution</td></tr>
<tr><td colspan="2">Substitution is a resource of cohesion whereby a word refers back to a previous segment of the text, which it stands for in a new co-text, thus avoiding repetition.</td></tr>
<tr><td>System</td><td>Système</td></tr>
<tr><td colspan="2">A system is a set of choices in a network.</td></tr>
<tr><td>Systemic Functional Linguistics</td><td>Linguistique Systémique Fonctionnelle</td></tr>
<tr><td colspan="2">Systemic Functional Linguistics is a linguistic theory based on the work of Michael Halliday. In its early form, it was called Scale and Category Grammar.</td></tr>
<tr><td>Target</td><td>Cible</td></tr>
<tr><td colspan="2">Target is sometimes used as a participant in a verbal clause. It is the entity against whom the process is directed in processes of blame, criticism, or praise.</td></tr>
<tr><td>Tenor</td><td>Teneur</td></tr>
<tr><td colspan="2">Tenor is a function of register. It is that part of register that relates to the relationships between the protagonists in an exchange.</td></tr>
<tr><td>Text</td><td>Texte</td></tr>
<tr><td colspan="2">A text can be considered to be a rank at a higher level than the clause. It is made up of clauses or clause complexes.</td></tr>
<tr><td>Textual metafunction</td><td>Métafonction textuelle</td></tr>
</table>

<table>
<tr><td colspan="2">The textual metafunction is that part of meaning that deals with the way the clause is structured.</td></tr>
<tr><td>Textual theme</td><td>Thème textuel</td></tr>
<tr><td colspan="2">A textual theme is a non-obligatory theme that serves to link the clause to the rest of the text.</td></tr>
<tr><td>Thematic progression</td><td>Progression thématique</td></tr>
<tr><td colspan="2">Thematic progression is the way themes develop through a text. They can, for example, be derived from a previous theme (constant progression) or a previous rheme (linear progression).</td></tr>
<tr><td>Theme</td><td>Thème</td></tr>
<tr><td colspan="2">Theme is a function within the textual metafunction. It is the speaker's starting point for the clause.</td></tr>
<tr><td>Thing</td><td>Entité</td></tr>
<tr><td colspan="2">A thing is the entity that is encoded in the head of a nominal group.</td></tr>
<tr><td>Token</td><td>Signe</td></tr>
<tr><td colspan="2">The token is a participant in an identifying relational process. It is the entity that is identified by the process.</td></tr>
<tr><td>Topical theme</td><td>Thème topical</td></tr>
<tr><td colspan="2">A topical theme is the first main component (subject, circumstantial adjunct, predicator or complement) of the clause. It constitutes the speaker's starting point for the clause.</td></tr>
<tr><td>Transitivity</td><td>Transitivité</td></tr>
<tr><td colspan="2">Transitivity is the major function of the ideational metafunction. It concerns the relationship between a process, the participants in the process, and, if there are any, the attendant circumstances.</td></tr>
<tr><td>Value</td><td>Valeur</td></tr>
<tr><td colspan="2">A value is a participant in an identifying relational clause. It is the entity used to identify the token.</td></tr>
<tr><td>Verb</td><td>Verbe</td></tr>
<tr><td colspan="2">A verb is the central word of the verbal group. It encodes a process.</td></tr>
<tr><td>Verbal process</td><td>Procès verbal</td></tr>
<tr><td colspan="2">A verbal process is a process of communication.</td></tr>
<tr><td>Verbiage</td><td>Parole</td></tr>
<tr><td colspan="2">The verbiage is a participant in a verbal process. It gives the content of the message being communicated.</td></tr>
<tr><td>Word</td><td>Mot</td></tr>
<tr><td colspan="2">A word is a constituent of a group.</td></tr>
</table>

References

Banks, David (2003a): "A note on modality in French", *Word*, 54:3, 325–334.

Banks, David (2003b): "Relativity as an antidote to incorrect linguistic analysis", in Delmas, Claude (ed.): *Correct, incorrect en linguistique anglaise* (CIEREC Travaux 113), Saint-Etienne, Publications de l'Université de Saint-Etienne, 13–23.

Banks, David (2005): *Introduction à la linguistique systémique de l'anglais*, Paris, L'Harmattan.

Banks, David (2009a): "Ce mot se: un pronom qui n'en est point", in Banks, David, Simon Eason & Janet Ormrod (eds.): *La linguistique systémique fonctionnelle et la langue française*, Paris, L'Harmattan, 177–193.

Banks, David (2009b): "The position of ideology in a systemic functional model", *Word*, 60, 39–63.

Banks, David (2010a): "The true nature of the French word *se*", in Swain, Elizabeth (ed.): *Thresholds and Potentialities of Systemic Functional Linguistics: Multlingual, Multimodal and Other Specialised Discourses*, Trieste, Edizioni Università di Trieste, 69–84.

Banks, David (2010b): "The interpersonal metafunction in French from a systemic functional perspective", *Language Sciences*, 32:3, 395–407.

Banks, David (2013): "The choice of grammatical metaphor in French political tracts", in O'Grady, Gerard, Tom Bartlett & Lise Fontaine (eds.): *Choice in Language: Applications in Text Analysis*, Sheffield, Equinox, 111–124.

Caffarel, Alice (2004): "Metafunctional profile of the grammar of French", in Caffarel, Alice, J.R. Martin & Christian M.I.M. Matthiessen (eds.): *Language Typology, a Functional Perspective*, Amsterdam, John Benjamins, 77–137.

Caffarel, Alice (2006): *A Systemic Functional Grammar of French, from Grammar to Discourse*, London, Continuum.

Fawcett, Robin (2000): *A Theory of Syntax for Systemic Functional Linguistics*, Amsterdam, John Benjamins.

Halliday, M.A.K. (1988): "On the language of physical science", in Ghadessy, M. (ed.): *Registers of Written English: Situational Factors and Linguistic Features*, London, Pinter, 162–178. [reprinted in Halliday, M.A.K. & J.R. Martin (1993): *Writing Science: Literacy and Discursive Power*, London, The Falmer Press,

54–68; and Halliday, M.A.K. (ed. Jonathan Webster) (2004): *The Language of Science*, London, Continuum, 140–158].

Halliday, M.A.K. (rev. Christian M.I.M. Matthiessen) (2014): *Halliday's Introduction to Functional Grammar*, 4th. edn. London, Arnold.

Halliday, M.A.K. & J.R. Martin (1993): *Writing Science: Literacy and Discursive Power*, London, Falmer Press.

Martin, J.R. & P.R.R. White (2005): *The Language of Evaluation: Appraisal in English*, Basingstoke, Palgrave Macmillan.

Rowlett, Paul (2007): *The Syntax of French*, Cambridge, Cambridge University Press.

Index